To Quench Our Thirst

To Quench Our Thirst

The Present and Future Status
of Freshwater Resources
of the United States

David A. Francko and

Robert G. Wetzel

Ann Arbor

The University of Michigan Press

1986 1985 1984 1983   4 3 2 1

Library of Congress Cataloging in Publication Data
Francko, David A.
      To quench our thirst.

      Includes bibliographical references and index.
      1. Water-supply—United States. I. Wetzel, Robert G.
II. Title.
TD223.F7 1983   333.91′211′0973   83-1071
ISBN 0-472-10032-7
ISBN 0-472-08037-7 (pbk.)

Preface

Water is a fundamentally important resource because it is essential for survival, because its use underlies all agricultural and industrial processes, and because it cannot be substituted for technologically. Water resource crises are not new to the late twentieth century, but have existed as long as man has banded together in concentrated settlements. History is rife with examples of cultural and societal decline caused directly or indirectly by freshwater limitations. Many of the historical attitudes about water which led to these water crises still exist in contemporary American society, leading in large measure to our current situation.

United States society faces acute and chronic water resource crises of major dimensions, which threaten our quality of life, state of individual freedoms, and position as a world leader. In our homes, in agriculture, and in industry, we currently use much more water than is being resupplied to usable sources through natural processes. Our explosive societal growth is rapidly degrading extant supplies and reducing the effectiveness of natural water recharge mechanisms. The uncertainties of climatic change dictate that we may have even less usable water in the future. As a society, we retain faith in the erroneous notions that fresh water is a resource without limit and that technological fixes can and will solve all our water resource problems. To continue our uncontrolled consumption and degradation of water is to invite inevitable water crises and equally inevitable societal decline in the coming decades.

The future need not be grim. We can learn from the lessons of past cultures, recognizing our problems and acting to solve them. By purely voluntary means and with no losses of real economic productivity, we can markedly reduce our consumption of water and the degradation of existing supplies. We can maximize the effectiveness of natural processes which recharge surface and groundwater reserves. Residential, agricultural, and industrial processes can, with existing technology, be made both cost-effective and water-efficient. The duality of water and energy limitations must be brought to the forefront of individual and governmental policy and actions. As a society, we must irrevocably and completely abandon our long-standing frontier ethic, recognizing the real economic value and the preciousness of liquid water.

We must progress beyond our resource-intensive cultural adolescence into stable societal maturity in what will surely be a resource-limited future. To defer action now is to invite the intervention of natural processes which will inexorably work to balance the water supply and demand equation, with catastrophic consequences to our nation and the millions throughout the world who depend on us for sustenance.

Our future is still in our hands. How will we respond to the challenge?

Contents

1 The Current Water Crisis

Conceal a flaw, and the world will imagine the worst.
Quintilian

Nearly every recent television newscast or magazine and newspaper edition carries a story about some new water-related crisis in America. What were once isolated instances of water shortfalls or gross water contamination are now common occurrences. We are currently entering an era in which cheap, clean, and plentiful water may cease to exist in much of the United States. The water crisis we now face is much more complex than the oversimplified menace of water pollution which has garnered attention in recent years. We are experiencing a syndrome of diverse, interrelated events which threaten to dwarf the energy crisis in potential significance and overall severity. In this book, we will examine the scientific, political, and historic basis of water-related problems in America. Our remarks are aimed at general readers and technically oriented individuals alike who believe that our current water problems will either go away on their own or be swept away solely by government action.

On the positive side, our sixty thousand local water agencies have for years delivered an abundance of clean, safe water to American consumers. Waterborne diseases are largely a thing of the past. Nonetheless, events in this nation are moving in such a way as to threaten the security of America's water future. The evidence is all around us. A farmer on the High Plains of Oklahoma surveys his parched fields, realizing to his chagrin that the irrigation water he so desperately needs has become too expensive to pump from depleted, overdrawn groundwater wells. Californians are embroiled in bitter disputes over vital water rights. At stake are the futures of the Los Angeles Basin and a major river system and prime agricultural regions to the north. It is the type of dispute in which we increasingly see no winners. Along the Gulf Coast and much of the eastern seaboard, people drawing water for morning coffee discover that their tapwater is brackish; saline ocean water has intruded into depleted groundwater stores of fresh water.

In nearly every state, bans on residential water use, which used to occur infrequently and only during severe summer droughts, are now commonplace events. Many large cities, particularly on the East Coast, are experiencing chronic water shortages due to a combination of high demand, overdrawn supplies, and antiquated leaking water delivery systems which frequently waste more water than they deliver.

In Connecticut, townspeople steeped in a long tradition of Yankee independence are forced to swallow their pride and import bottled drinking water from neighboring communities to replace chemical-laden municipal supplies. The evacuation of whole communities in upstate New York is contemplated when it is discovered that an abandoned chemical dump has poisoned the groundwater, turning neighborhoods into veritable sewers. Soon, similar dumps are uncovered in hundreds of locations across the country, and no one really knows the long-term effects they will have on precious groundwater supplies. Michigan, billed as the Great Lakes State, is inundated with groundwater contamination, so much so that even a state blessed with bountiful freshwater resources ponders the future with trepidation. People laugh as they see an evening news report on a river in Ohio so laden with flammable pollutants that it catches fire. The laughter subsides, however, when they realize that similar situations probably occur in their own communities. Acid precipitation has turned regional lake districts throughout New England and Canada into a series of water bodies devoid of fish. Residents are told to waste tap water for five minutes each morning to flush home plumbing of metal residues that have been dissolved from pipes by acidic groundwater.

In Florida, rock strata depleted of groundwater slump downward, causing great sinkholes which swallow whole neighborhoods. We see an increased incidence of devastating floods and massive erosion of irreplaceable farmland as farmers abandon wise, post–Dust Bowl land use practices, wetlands are drained, and natural buffer areas are denuded or paved with asphalt.

The water crunch, in all its varied manifestations, is upon us. From the standpoint of water availability, our nation is drying, and it may become a good deal dryer in the future. We continue to withdraw and redistribute water from existing supplies faster than it is replaced by natural processes. The resupply of water to surface and groundwater reserves may abate in coming years due to climatic change and man-induced alterations in the landscape. Water supplies which do exist are being rapidly degraded by processes which are, in many cases, essentially irreversible. These problems have not appeared overnight. Conflicts over water have been a part of the American scene for decades in chronically water-poor regions like the West. It is the nature and widespread magnitude of our current situation that distinguishes it from the past, and demands our immediate attention.

We are at the crossroads in our water economy. The actions we take in coming years will have far-reaching effects. We cannot substitute other commodities for liquid water as we can for oil. Water is physiologically essential to our survival. It subsidizes, directly or indirectly, all agricultural and industrial outputs. Because water is such a basic necessity and is used so intensively, a long-term water crisis of major proportions would affect all levels of our society, eroding our standard of living and our national position as a world leader.

This grim scenario can and must be averted. Although we face the near certainty of a chronically water-limited American society, the future need not be disastrous. If our problems are addressed now, in a comprehensive manner, we can ease the transition into water limitation, using existing technology, with minimal perturbations in economic or social stability. If we defer this essential action, opting instead to allow events to run their course, we face at best an uncertain future. Inflammatory rhetoric, scare tactics, and doomsday predictions are ineffective weapons in environmental crises, because they galvanize schisms between opposing groups and short-circuit meaningful change.

How can we understand and deal with the complexities of our current water problems and cope with future crises? First, we must accept water crises for what they are: *complex, multifaceted syndromes of events, comprised of scientific, social, and political components, brought about by the collective actions of individuals, industry, agriculture, and government.* By definition, our current water problems are not solvable by quick technological fixes or solely through governmental intervention. They must be understood in a comprehensive manner and solved by the collective actions of individual citizens, corporate and agricultural entities, and government.

For simplicity, current water problems can be divided into two functional groups: (1) problems in water supply and demand, and (2) problems in the degradation of water supplies and of the terrestrial environment necessary for effecting water supply recharge. As we shall see, these two groups are not mutually exclusive, but the dichotomy is useful for discussion and forms the basis for the succeeding narrative.

Supply and demand problems occur when, for a number of reasons, human use of water exceeds the supply of readily extractable water in a given area. To understand supply and demand problems, we must understand the dynamics of liquid water in the environment and how man influences the movement of water in the hydrological cycle.

The degradation of water supplies occurs in two ways. First, man adds solid, liquid, or gaseous pollutants to the air, water, or land and these contaminants eventually find their way to stored water supplies. Second, man can alter the terrestrial landscape, so that erosion and other processes overload aquatic systems with silt, nutrients, and soil-borne contaminants. The rate of movement of water from sources to eventual flow to the oceans is also accelerated, reducing the recharge of groundwater supplies.

In this book we discuss both of these broad classes of water-related problems. We will examine the specific aspects of our present acute crises in America and the ramifications for the future. But it is not enough to look only at the present and the immediate past. The historical development of water crises in America and the obvious parallels between our problems and those faced by other societies in the past must be understood as we tread the same deadly pathway. We will close with scenarios of two possible future Americas, one in which we abdicate our responsibilities to deal with water problems and a much preferable scenario based on a sane approach to water problem solving in the years ahead.

After examining the evidence, it should be clear that there are no easy choices, no quick answers in the path to a secure water future. However, the answers *are* available to use if we are willing to make the hard choices they entail. In this book, we can do no more than summarize some of the myriad things we can do at all levels of society to prevent a water limitation in the decades ahead, which promises to be as painful as the energy crisis of the 1970s, from which America has still not fully recovered.

Sound choices in water strategies can only be made by an educated public, capable of sifting fact from fancy and wishful thinking from pragmatic reality. It is to this broad audience that we direct our discussion.

2 The Dynamics of Fresh Water in the United States

Each person requires only about 2 liters of water each day to meet their physiological needs. One might think that our seemingly abundant water supplies should more than adequately meet these needs, despite the large size of the present population. We use, however, much more water than our minimal 2 liters per day. On the average, including the water used by agriculture and industry to produce food and goods for our consumption, each person uses about 1,500 liters of water per day.

The fresh water we need for survival is drawn from a system of usable sources which occur both on the surface and below ground. The amount of water stored in these sources is not static, but varies through time. Simply stated, a water shortage develops when humans withdraw more water from supplies stored in a given region than is being resupplied by natural processes. Several key points are essential to an understanding of the causes and potential solutions of these man-induced water supply problems.

First, water *moves* through the biosphere. Water present in usable sources is constantly being replenished and renewed by natural recharge processes driven by atmospheric precipitation. The recharge rate of a given water source is highly variable and influenced by a number of factors. Importantly, this recharge rate dictates the absolute limits to which a given water source can be used without danger of overdraft. As we shall see, ignorance or disregard of these fundamental limits have resulted in both acute and chronic water supply problems in much of the United States.

Second, water supplies are unevenly distributed across the United States. When human, industrial, or agricultural developments are con-

5

centrated because of other desirable environmental characteristics in regions chronically poor in water, water crises commonly develop. The asymmetry between the distribution of water demand and water supplies is the basis of many of our contemporary regional problems.

Third, the movement of water in the biosphere, the so-called hydrological cycle, is itself a dynamic process, influenced both by the activities of man and by factors beyond man's control. This dynamism dictates that both the total amount of water available to the United States and its relative distribution may be fundamentally altered in the years ahead.

Water in Our Biosphere

Although water is fundamentally abundant on earth, over 99 percent of it rests in the oceans (table 1). Ocean water is highly saline, making it unpalatable for direct consumption. Further, removal of salt is an energy-consumptive process that is not very practical for large-scale use. Desalination of seawater can provide only limited amounts of fresh water in certain areas where solar energy is consistently high. Glacial or polar ice is simply not a practical source of fresh water. The reservoirs of water in the oceans and polar ice are large but their recycling times are long, i.e., it takes many thousands of years for inputs from all sources to replace losses by all processes (see table 1). For all practical purposes then, surface and groundwater supplies constitute the only major sources of exploitable fresh water available to us.

Of the fresh water associated with land, most water occurs in groundwater, that water occupying voids in geological rock and soil strata. Most of the remaining water occurs in freshwater lakes and rivers. A small but very important amount occurs in water vapor in the atmosphere. The renewal or recharge times of these freshwater reservoirs will be emphasized again and again in this chapter. The renewal times of groundwater sources are slow, on the average replaced every three hundred years by natural processes. If man removes a significant portion of a groundwater reservoir, replacement of that supply takes a considerable amount of time.

The renewal times of freshwater lakes are more rapid than those of groundwater reservoirs. Lake renewal times, however, are highly variable depending on the characteristics of their watersheds, their basin shape, and the climate of the region in which they occur. If water is

TABLE 1   Water in the Biosphere

Water Source	Volume (thousands of km³)	Percentage of Total	Renewal Time
Oceans	1,370,000	97.61	37,000 years[a]
Polar ice glaciers	29,000	2.08	16,000 years
Groundwater (actively exchanged)[b]	4,000	0.29	300 years
Freshwater lakes	125	0.009	1–100 years[c]
Saline lakes	104	0.008	10–1,000 years[c]
Soil and subsoil moisture	67	0.005	280 days
Rivers	1.2	0.00009	12–20 days[d]
Atmospheric water vapor	14	0.0009	9 days

Source: J. R. Vallentyne, "Freshwater Supplies and Pollution: Effects of the Demophoric Explosion on Water and Man," in *The Environmental Future,* ed. N. Polunin (London: Macmillan and Co., 1972), p. 186.

a. Based on net evaporation from the oceans.

b. Kalinin and Bykov (1969) estimated that the total groundwater to a depth of 5 km in the earth's crust amounts to 60×10^6 km³. This is much greater than the estimate by the U.S. Geological Survey of 8.3×10^6 km³ to a depth of 4 km. Only the volume of the upper, actively exchanged groundwater is included here. G. P. Kalinin and V. D. Bykov, "The World's Water Resources, Present and Future," *Impact of Science on Technology* 19, no. 2 (1969):135–50.

c. Renewal times for lakes vary directly with volume and mean depth, and inversely with rate of discharge. The absolute range for saline lakes is from days to thousands of years.

d. Twelve days for rivers with relatively small catchment areas of less than 100,000 km²; twenty days for major rivers draining directly to the sea.

removed from a lake or if that lake becomes polluted, it takes considerable time for the water to be replenished or the contaminants removed from the basin (if it occurs at all) once the pollution has stopped.

The approximate distribution of water in the continental United States, shown in table 2, indicates that over 85 percent of all water occurs in storage in groundwater aquifers (col. 1). The remaining water occurs in surface reservoirs. The volume of water in each of these storage reservoirs that is removed and replaced within each reservoir each year (col. 2) is highly variable. The important parameter to note is that the annual replacement values (col. 3 = 1/2) are also highly variable as a result. Thus, for example, only about 3 percent of total water circulation stored in the large groundwater reserve is replaced each year. This slow replacement value dictates that if significant proportions of stored groundwater are removed by man, recharge often is not rapid. The amount of reserve water in surface waters and the atmosphere is much more variable and affected to a greater extent by differing annual rainfall than is groundwater.

The Hydrological Cycle

Water moves from the atmosphere, is stored temporarily on land and in the groundwater, and flows to the primary reservoir, the oceans. The hydrological cycle consists of evaporation, precipitation, and surface and groundwater runoff. Each phase involves transport, temporary storage, and a shift in the state of the water—a cycle which dictates the extent to which water becomes available for man's use.

Water evaporates into the atmosphere from liquid precipitation itself while it is falling; from the oceans, lakes, and streams; from soils; and by transpiration of plants. Evaporation rates are controlled by many environmental parameters. Atmospheric vapor, although a small portion of the total water reserves, is stored for the least amount of time (averaging about nine days) before returning to land or oceans as rain, snow, sleet, hail, and condensates (dew and frost).

TABLE 2   Distribution of Water in the Continental United States

	(1) Volume		(2) Annual Circulation	(3) Replacement Period
	$\times 10^9$ m³	%	($\times 10^9$ m³/year)	(in years)
Liquid water				
Groundwater				
Shallow (<800 m deep)	63,000	43.2%	310	>200
Deep (>800 m deep)	63,000	43.2	6.2	>10,000
Freshwater lakes	19,000	13.0	190	100
Soil moisture (1-m root zone)	630	0.43	3,100	0.2
Salt lakes	58	0.04	5.7	>10
Average in stream channels	50	0.03	1,900	<0.03
Water vapor in atmosphere	190	0.13	6,200	>0.03
Frozen water, glaciers	67	0.05	1.6	>40

Source: Ad Hoc Panel on Hydrology, *Scientific Hydrology* (Washington, D.C.: Federal Council for Science and Technology, 1962), p. 37.

The precipitated water may be intercepted or transpired by plants, may run off over and through the ground to streams (surface runoff), or may infiltrate the ground (fig. 1). Up to 80 percent of the intercepted water and surface water is returned directly to the atmosphere by evaporation (see table 1). Hence, only a small portion of incoming precipitation becomes actively involved in water recharge processes. Water that infiltrates may be temporarily stored (renewal times of 70 to 280 days) as soil moisture or transpired by plants. Some of the water percolates to deeper soil zones and is stored as groundwater (average renewal time of 200 to 300 years). Groundwater is actively exchanged and may be used by plants, flow out as springs, or seep into streams and lakes as runoff.

Groundwater and surface water runoff characteristics are extremely complex and variable from place to place because of plant uptake, great variability in soil composition and layering, and variations in climate.[1] Each of the runoff processes from rainfall or meltwater respond differently to variations in topography, soil, and characteristics of precipitation, and indirectly to variations in climate, vegetation, and land use patterns. As a result, runoff flow processes influence the volume, periodicity, and chemical characteristics of receiving streams and lakes.

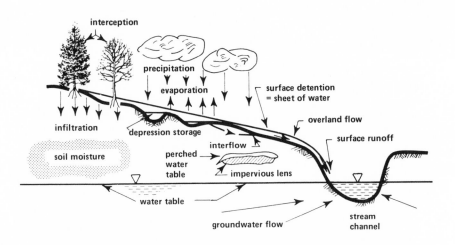

Fig. 1.   Major pathways of the runoff phases of the hydrological cycle. (Adapted from D. M. Grey, ed., *Handbook on the Principles of Hydrology* [Ottawa, Ont.: National Research Council Canada, 1970], fig. 4-1.)

Groundwater Characteristics and Distribution

The largest available source of fresh water occurs underground. Groundwater refers to water that fills all of the voids within a geological stratum.[2] The groundwater zone is saturated with water. Unsaturated, aerated zones usually occur above the saturated groundwater zones and extend upward to the ground surface.

Water enters soil and clings to soil particles by capillary forces. The spaces between soil particles are mixed with air and water. As water settles further and reaches an area of impermeable rock, all spaces are filled with water—the upper surface of this water-saturated soil is the *water table*. Geological formations containing sufficient saturated permeable material to provide significant quantities of water to wells and springs are called *aquifers*. Aquifers usually overlie impermeable geological rock material which restricts water to the more permeable stratum. Examples of such confining strata include clays and granite. The type of stratum in which the aquifer is located determines its usefulness as a water source to man.

Many types of geological formations serve as aquifers. Most aquifers (about 90 percent) occur in unconsolidated rock such as gravel and sand. Many of these aquifers occur in old valleys and river beds from past periods of glaciation or near existing streams where water infiltrates from the stream into the nearby groundwater. Other aquifers occur in limestone deposits where part of the rock has dissolved and water accumulates in cracks and fractures. Certain volcanic rocks from basaltic lava flows are permeable and hold significant aquifers, but these are generally small compared to unconsolidated rock formations.

The aquifers, then, are effectively large underground storage reservoirs in which water enters from the ground surface in a recharge area, often some distance from the main groundwater aquifer. Water in the aquifer flows by gravity until it reaches some place where the water table intersects the surface or encounters a fracture to emerge as a spring. Of course, wells remove water from aquifers artificaly. Under ordinary conditions the amount of water removed or replaced each year represents only a small portion of the total storage capacity. However, in many regions of the United States, water is being removed from aquifers much faster than they are being recharged.

Groundwater Movement

Groundwater is generally flowing within the underground rock strata holding it. Flow of groundwater is important for many reasons. Under natural conditions, surface water derived largely from precipitation flows by gravity to lower strata until it encounters more impermeable strata and saturates all pores of the rock strata. Water moves horizontally as more water enters from above, is dispersed, and eventually flows to some point where the water table intersects the ground surface, such as at a stream or lake. Soluble materials dissolve into the water as it moves through the rock—some rocks such as limestone are much more soluble than others (e.g., clays or granite). Pollutants added by the activities of man to the atmosphere or to the surface waters seeping into groundwater are often carried with the water to points very distant from where they entered the ground. Under natural conditions, groundwater moves slowly (2 meters/day to 2 meters/year),[3] depending on local differences in hydrogeological conditions; hence pollutants can be interred in groundwater for many decades and be transported far from sites of origin.

When man artificially extracts groundwater from aquifers, the flows within the aquifers are altered. As water is removed by a well, the water table in that area is lowered and water flows from surrounding parts of the aquifer into the cone-shaped region where water content is less. The rate at which the region can be replenished depends on many factors, including the porosity characteristics of the rock of the aquifer, the position of the well in the aquifer in relation to its boundaries, and rate of groundwater recharge from surface sources.

Groundwater Levels and Capacities

Groundwater levels within aquifers vary over time in response to a number of factors. Any phenomenon that produces a difference between supply and withdrawal will change the groundwater level.[4]

Seasonal fluctuations of groundwater levels often result from seasonal variations in rainfall and removal of water for periodic uses such as irrigation. If the ground is frozen, seepage recharge is lowest in winter and is highest in spring at snowmelt. Low groundwaters often are found in the fall at the end of the irrigation season. Utilization of soil water by plants with losses to the atmosphere through evapotranspiration can seasonally depress the water table levels as the rate of plant growth increases to its maximum.

Over short periods of several years, rainfall is not an accurate indicator of groundwater recharge. The time required by rainwater to reach shallow aquifers can be short (minutes to days); in these situations recharge of shallow groundwater reservoirs can closely follow rainfall patterns. But most aquifers are deep and underlie soils of low permeabilities, where recharge flows can take months or years to reach the aquifers. Depression of groundwater levels during seasonally drier periods often results from increased extraction by pumping. This groundwater drawdown becomes particularly acute during a series of dry years in which rainfall is below the mean for a long period.

Finally, the importance of urbanization to groundwater supplies must be noted. Shallow-water aquifers are usually adequate for water supplies in low-demand, rural areas where individual wells are used for each home or need. As populations increase, public water supplies shift to deep aquifer sources. Much of the ground surface is covered with impermeable materials (e.g., asphalt, buildings) which greatly reduce percolation. Storm sewers remove much of incoming precipitation and carry it to places far away from the groundwater aquifers beneath the metropolitan areas. Similarly, water removed for domestic and industrial purposes from groundwater aquifers is used, often loaded with inorganic and organic compounds, and moved some distance away from its sources for treatment and disposal. As a result, the aquifers of many metropolitan areas are continually depressed by extraction exceeding recharge.

Aquifer Distribution

The distribution of aquifers in the continental United States shown in figure 2 indicates the regions where significant supplies of groundwater occur.[5] Regions with good groundwater supplies do not always coincide with corresponding patterns of human water demand. The blank areas indicate regions where yield from wells is very low (less than 3 liters/second). Ten major groundwater regions can be delineated on the basis of their capacity to retain groundwater (regions numbered as in fig. 2).

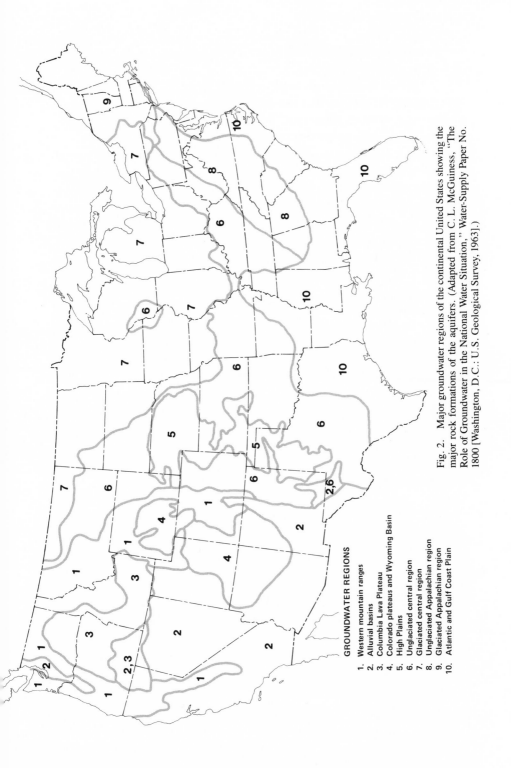

GROUNDWATER REGIONS

1. Western mountain ranges
2. Alluvial basins
3. Columbia Lava Plateau
4. Colorado plateaus and Wyoming Basin
5. High Plains
6. Unglaciated central region
7. Glaciated central region
8. Unglaciated Appalachian region
9. Glaciated Appalachian region
10. Atlantic and Gulf Coast Plain

Fig. 2. Major groundwater regions of the continental United States showing the major rock formations of the aquifers. (Adapted from C. L. McGuiness, "The Role of Groundwater in the National Water Situation," Water-Supply Paper No. 1800 [Washington, D.C.: U.S. Geological Survey, 1963].)

Regions of Low Groundwater Capacities

1. In the western mountain ranges the rocks are dense and much of the precipitation is not absorbed but flows to valleys and away from the region. Wells are only practical in valleys and most water supply needs are met by small surface reservoirs.
2. The intermountain alluvial basins contain erosional rock and store water from the adjacent highlands. The climate in this region is arid and in this region withdrawal of groundwater for irrigation and domestic uses from naturally high-yielding aquifers now exceeds their recharge. The storage capacity is rapidly being depleted.
4. The Colorado plateaus and Wyoming Basin region contains relatively low water-bearing aquifers. The sandstone and shale deposits that predominate much of the region are often high and relatively dry.
6. In the unglaciated central region of plains and plateaus, most aquifers occur in limestone and sandstone of relatively low yield. Good aquifers occur only in alluvial deposits adjacent to major rivers. Many areas in this region contain very poor aquifers of low or salty water.
9. The glaciated Appalachian region contains relatively thin deposits of weathered rock and glacial drift. As a result, in much of the region the aquifer yield is low; most are restricted to sand and gravel deposits on outwash plains and near stream channels.

Regions of Moderate Groundwater Capacities

5. The High Plains region extends eastward from the Rocky Mountains and contains the major geological Ogallala formation of rock alluvium that is up to 150 meters in thickness. Although the sand and gravel of aquifers in this semiarid region contain high-yielding groundwater storage, recharge is slow because of extremely low precipitation. Water tables in this region are declining rapidly as use of this stored water exceeds recharge.
8. In the unglaciated Appalachian region the geological deposits are highly variable and relatively good groundwater areas occur in small, localized areas from drainage from surrounding hills. In other areas only small yields can be obtained from sandstone and shale deposits.

Regions of High Groundwater Capacities

3. In the Columbia lava plateau, water from the surrounding mountains enters aquifers of volcanic lava flows, alluvium, and former
   lake sediments. Groundwater supplies are relatively large, especially in river valley areas.
7. The glaciated central region contains much fine-grained sand and
   gravel deposited by outwash from the major continental glaciers
   to thicknesses often more than 300 meters. Groundwater aquifers
   in this region are generally high-yielding and adequately recharged
   at the present time.
10. In the Atlantic and Gulf coastal plain, massive deposits of sedi-
   mentary rock (sand, gravel, limestone) occur to great thicknesses.
   The aquifers are extensive and productive. Because of the intensive
   use of groundwater by great concentrations of people in this area,
   removal often exceeds recharge and results in seawater intrusion
   and land subsidence in certain areas.

Surface Waters

The landscape of our continent was shaped to a great extent by
the slow but nonetheless catastrophic events of the last major glaciation.
This powerful force reshaped previous landforms to varying extents. A
great deal of reshaping occurred in the central and midwestern regions
where rock formations are less resistant, while less took place in the
eastern and western portions of granitic and basaltic rock of mountain
ranges. As the glaciers melted and gradually retreated some ten to
fifteen thousand years ago, glacial meltwaters further modified the landscape by massive erosion and deposition of rock and debris originally
incorporated into the glaciers as they formed and moved southward.

Most of the major river systems of the northern part of the United
States were formed by this last glaciation. In addition, thousands of
lakes were formed by the gouging activities of the glaciers and by blocks
of ice that were left in depressions as the glaciers receded. Because the
last Wisconsin Glaciation Period was less well developed and active
than previous glaciations, this ice movement extended across most of
Canada but did not move far southward into the continental United
States. As a result, most of the extant natural lakes are disproportion-
ately concentrated into the northern tier of states and are particularly

abundant in Minnesota, Wisconsin, Michigan, the northern parts of adjacent southern states, and in northern states extending eastward to the coast of New England. The greatest legacy of this glacial activity is the Great Lakes, five major lakes that collectively contain about 20 percent of the fresh water on the surface of the world.[6]

In addition to the formation of this large lake district in the northern states, less numerous but important lakes and river systems were formed by the movements of rock formations and volcanic activity of mountain ranges in the East and especially the extensive Rocky Mountain and smaller coastal mountain ranges of the West and Northwest. Small glaciers in the higher mountain ranges also scoured out many lake systems.

Basic differences occur in the underlying rock formations beneath the lake and river systems. In more mountainous regions of the West, Northwest, and large sections of the Northeast, the underlying rock is hard and relatively impermeable to water. Water inputs from rainfall and snowmelt pass through relatively thin soils, move relatively rapidly to lower elevations, and dissolve low amounts of nutrients and other chemicals from the associated soil and rock formations. In the southern central Midwest and much of the rest of the United States where complex rock formations exist, soils are more permeable and deeper, and percolating waters contain higher concentrations of dissolved nutrients and other chemical compounds. These geological differences result not only in different groundwater retention capacities and renewal rates between the regions, but also in different susceptibilities of surface and groundwaters to change in water quality from man's activities.

Drainage Basin Characteristics

Recall that the processes of water economy in the hydrological cycle affect the distribution and movement of water. Evaporation from the oceans, because of their much larger surface area (three-fourths of the earth's surface), is greater than from land. Precipitation is greater onto land masses than on the oceans. The drainage characteristics of various landforms determine the rapidity with which water ultimately returns to the ocean. Man's activities fundamentally alter drainage basin characteristics, thereby directly altering, usually for the worse, a given region's hydrological cycle.

Once water is returned to the land by precipitation, it either evaporates or is absorbed by soil, and moves. An obvious but often overlooked fact is the simple operation of *gravity*. Water moves downhill from points of inception and eventually to the ocean. Within a lake ecosystem, water passes through soil, some evaporating and being used by plants, some passing into groundwater, and some collecting in rivulets and eventually streams. The tributaries collect into streams and enter the depression of a lake basin or reservoir. While groundwater flow rates are generally slow and the pathways long, flow to lakes is rapid and retention times in lakes are generally short (six to seven years on the average).[7]

As water enters a lake basin, water velocity slows. As a result, the energy of the moving water dissipates, permitting much of suspended particulate matter to settle within the lake basin. The greater water residence time within the lake basin allows biological processes to operate on imported materials for longer periods of time and in a different environment than was the case in streams. The lake, then, functions as both a settling basin and a biologically active site for further use of the materials that were not completely utilized or cycled during the transport from the soils through the streams and groundwaters before reaching the lakes.

Natural lakes, as well as man-made reservoir systems, are greatly influenced by the vegetation and soil characteristics of the drainage basin (watershed) surrounding them. The vegetation, whether consisting of forest trees or herbaceous vegetation or both, as well as plant litter on the ground surface, intercepts precipitation much more efficiently than bare ground.[8] This plant material reduces the kinetic energy of falling rainwater and water flowing downhill and alters the chemical composition of the incoming water.[9] Thus vegetation both minimizes soil erosion and regulates nutrient flow to water leaving the soil to streams and recipient lakes. If the watershed is stressed by, for example, pollution, deforestation, or road building, not only is the water flow altered but these conditions change the nutrient flux and cycling within the terrestrial part of the ecosystem and losses to waters. These losses are gains to receiving streams and lakes and affect the quality of those waters in ways that often make them less desirable for man's uses.

The transition of water from the terrestrial landscape to the lake is a tortuous route. Chemicals, particularly those without a gaseous phase, such as calcium, magnesium, or potassium, are largely transported into and out of ecosystems by moving water.[10] Other chemicals, such as nitrogen, phosphorus, and organic compounds largely in soluble form, are much more dynamic and influenced by the biota not only in the soil, but also in the streams, especially by organisms associated with the stream sediments, such as bacteria or algae.

As inflow collects and flows toward a lake basin, the stream slows in velocity as the elevation gradient declines. In the gradient transition from upland parts of the watershed down to the lake itself, the interface region between the two components is often occupied by extensive wetlands. This wetland interface zone consists of plants that are among the most productive of any in the world, often exceeding growth rates of man's best-growing agricultural crops and exceeding growth of the densest tropical forests. The wetlands and the extensive shoreline vegetation in littoral zones of many lakes do more than simply grow well. The intensive metabolism of the communities in the wetlands and littoral areas of streams and lakes effectively regulate and control the loading rates of nutrients and particulate matter entering the water bodies from the land.

One finds, then, two types of natural buffering systems within most aquatic drainage basins. The forest-herbaceous vegetation and the wetland-littoral vegetation systems both function in complex ways to recycle efficiently the nutrients available within their habitats and regulate the release of these compounds to the downslope streams and lake. Great improvements in our recent understanding of the operation of these ecosystem components have shown not only how important they are to surface water quality and groundwater recharge capacities, but also that man's activities must carefully alter these systems if any part is to be exploited. Otherwise, the ability of these ecosystem parts to respond, recover, or change following disturbances can be easily exceeded.

Water within a lake basin or reservoir represents usable storage. Water retention times within basins are a result of the balance between inputs and losses. Inputs include precipitation on the lake surface, surface water influents from the drainage basin, and groundwater seepage into the lake through its sediments. Losses of water occur through a surface outflow through an outlet stream, by seepage through the basin walls, by evaporation directly from the surface, or through the emergent and floating-leaved plants.

Obviously, for a lake or reservoir to be a lake the water has to remain in the basin. Retention times vary greatly from a few days among some reservoirs that are functionally widening of rivers, to an average of six to seven years for natural lakes, to well over a hundred years for some lakes (e.g., Lake Michigan). Most lakes and reservoirs receive most of their water from surface influents, and the sediments of the basin itself form a relatively impermeable seal. As a result, the loading of chemicals and particulate matter from precipitation and the watershed, and their effects on the water quality, influence both how much chemical and particulate matter reaches the body of water and how long it remains there to be utilized and influence the organisms that can grow there.

Climate: The Unknown Factor in the Hydrological Cycle

As we have seen, solar energy and precipitation intercepted by land are driving forces of the hydrological cycle. The extent and characteristics of both ground and surface water supplies are directly influenced by the distribution and quantity of incoming rainfall. In the case of groundwater in particular, the amount of water presently in storage is a reflection of the prevailing rainfall pattern of the last several years and even decades.

The climatic processes which determine when and where rain will fall are not fixed in time. We know that climatic patterns over the continental United States seem to change in cyclical, decades-long patterns. Many climatologists now believe that the past several decades, the period of time when our current supply and use patterns were established, has been an abnormally wet, cool period.[11] The evidence indicates that we are currently entering a period of hotter, dryer weather more typical of the climate of the continental United States in the last several hundred years. If this prediction is true, and events of the last few years tend to indicate that it is, the actual amount of water in both surface and groundwater storage will decrease in the years ahead.

These climatic changes are apparently brought on by alterations in the path of prevailing high-altitude westerly winds as they sweep across the continent. A change in the direction of the westerlies changes the prevailing rainfall pattern markedly. If current theory is correct, such alterations in rainfall patterns would most greatly be noted in regions such as the Southwest and the High Plains, which are already poor in available water. Clearly, even a few dry years in a row could plunge these regions back into the Dust Bowl conditions of the 1930s.

Though it has an unpredictable nature and man has no direct control over it, the climatic factor is of immense importance in the hydrological cycle. We must be aware of the dangers inherent in predicting the future availability of water in the United States based on present supply estimates. While we cannot as yet determine the actual extent of future climatic fluctuations, we can be certain that inevitable changes will alter our water economy and availability.

NOTES

1. R. G. Wetzel, *Limnology* (Philadelphia: W. B. Saunders Co., 1975); M. J. Kirkby, ed., *Hillslope Hydrology* (New York: John Wiley and Sons, 1978).

2. D. K. Todd, *Groundwater Hydrology,* 2d ed. (New York: John Wiley and Sons, 1980); R. A. Freeze and J. A. Cherry, *Groundwater* (Englewood Cliffs, N.J.: Prentice-Hall, 1979).

3. Ibid.

4. Ibid.

5. Ibid. See also C. L. McGuinness, "The Role of Groundwater in the National Water Situation," Water-Supply Paper No. 1800 (Washington, D.C.: U.S. Geological Survey, 1963); *Groundwater in the Western Hemisphere,* Natural Resources/Water Series No. 4 (New York: United Nations, 1976); R. M. Cushman et al., *Sourcebook of Hydrologic and Ecological Features* (Ann Arbor: Ann Arbor Science Publishers, 1980).

6. Wetzel, *Limnology.*

7. Ibid.

8. Ibid.

9. An excellent example of one of the best-studied ecosystems is presented in G. E. Likens et al., *Biogeochemistry of a Forested Ecosystem* (New York: Springer-Verlag, 1977).

10. Ibid.

11. R. A. Bryson and T. J. Murray, *Climates of Hunger* (Madison: University of Wisconsin Press, 1977).

3 Water Supply and Demand Crises in Contemporary America

Who lin'd himself with hope,
Eating the air on primise of supply.

Shakespeare

So little in his purse, so much upon his back.

Joseph Hall

The reader who is aware of the basic processes which influence the extent and availability of surface and groundwaters in the United States is now in a better position to appreciate the specifics of the current water supply and demand crises. There is a finite limit to the amount of water which can be extracted per unit time from a given water source without depleting that source. We have seen that while much of our nation's water occurs in underground aquifers, groundwater recharge rate is generally very slow, rendering these sources inordinately prone to overdraft. Lastly, the distribution of usable water sources is not uniform. Rather, large regions of the continental United States are poorly endowed with either surface or groundwater.

It would be impossible in a book of this size to examine even a fraction of the water supply and demand problems which now plague the United States. Suffice it to say that every state in the nation has water problems dealing with inconsistencies between the supply of water and the demand for water. It is instructive, however, to look at some large-scale regional problem areas as examples of the general nature of these processes.

Usable water comprises one of the most important parts of a human society's resource base. Ecologists use the term *carrying capacity* to denote the maximum population size a given environment and its resource base can support. Human, plant, or bacterial populations cannot increase their numbers far beyond this maximal level. Inevitably, demand for limiting resources must decrease. In human populations, this decrease in demand has often been accomplished by such repugnant means as war, famine, plague, and mass exodus (see chap. 5).

When considering water as a limiting resource, we must be mindful of the many uses it has beyond physiological need. While each person requires 2 liters of water per day to fulfill physiological needs, we each consume about 1,500 liters per person per day through agriculture and industrial processes. The current water crisis is not only the result of population growth in the United States, it is also the result of explosive technological growth, both in the sense of per capita production and consumption, and in the sense that technology has permitted the growth of populations and their resource utilization to take place. To understand the current water consumption momentum of the man-machine system, we need to describe the combined effects of population in a biological sense and production-consumption in a technological sense.

The term *demophoric growth* encompasses both of these resource-consumptive processes.[1] This concept recognizes that resources are consumed both *directly* by man to satisfy physiological needs and to produce goods and *indirectly* through the use of produced goods. Demophoric growth predicts that as population and technology expand, resource utilization per capita increases exponentially rather than linearly. The net effect of explosive demophoric growth, which has characterized United States society since World War II, is that the environmental carrying capacity of a given region, determined by the presence of limiting resources like water, is reduced at an exponential rate.

Simply stated, many parts of the United States have already met or exceeded their environmental carrying capacity with regard to liquid water availability. It is this factor which makes chronic water shortfalls so dangerous. As noted, chronic resource limitation brought on by excessive demand cannot long continue; inevitably, consumption must decrease, whether voluntarily or through ecological constraints. Many regions of the United States are existing in a state where consumption is exceeding the water recharge rate of available sources, so that present demand is quenched by dipping into future reserves. If the climate does indeed change and become dryer, we will be in an even more tenuous position, because the environmental carrying capacity of these already water-poor regions will, by definition, be drastically reduced.

Let us examine in depth some specific, large-scale water supply and demand crisis regions in the United States. It should be noted that these regions by no means represent the only water overdraft regions in the United States; similar problems can be found locally and regionally in nearly every state.

The Arid West

While water overdraft is a problem common to many regions of contemporary America, the arid western half of the United States has been particularly hard hit. Very few natural lakes occur west of the Mississippi, and, with the exception of the Pacific Northwest, nearly all areas in this region rely on groundwater and sparse supplies in rivers and man-made reservoirs. Even in the best of times, the regional rainfall average of under 20 inches per year is barely adequate to recharge subsurface aquifers and stave off drought. From the days of John Wesley Powell (see chap. 5), we have been warned that water limitation would be the major factor constraining development of the American West.

While one-quarter of all the water used in the United States comes from groundwater aquifers, this percentage is much higher in the West. In West Texas, groundwater supplies 75 percent of the total water consumption. In Arizona, it supplies 62 percent of total consumption, and in California, about 40 percent.[2] The majority of water consumption in the region as a whole is used directly in irrigated agriculture. Irrigation water has made most areas of the arid West bloom, transforming the region from the High Plains to the San Joaquin Valley into a multibillion dollar agricultural complex of immense importance. Nearly all irrigation water must be pumped from wells tapped into extant aquifers, so that irrigation costs have escalated sharply with increased energy costs. Further, as aquifers are depleted, wells must be driven to greater depths, further increasing the cost of water delivery.

There is little question that to date, the expense of irrigation has been more than compensated for by agricultural output. Over 18 percent of total farm production ($16.6 billion; 1977 figures[3]) comes from the arid West, including 66 percent of the nation's cotton and 21 percent of its wheat. With the advent of the energy crisis, however, the water needs of agriculture have increasingly come into conflict with new residential and industrial water demands accruing from phenomenal human migration into the Sun Belt.

The West includes some of the fastest-growing metropolitan areas in the United States. Many communities experienced growth rates in excess of 25 percent between 1970 and 1980.[4] The demophoric growth of many of these cities is directly related to expansion of industry and technology based on the abundant supplies of exploitable energy reserves found in the region. The exploration for and extraction of gas, oil, and coal reserves requires huge amounts of water, much of it hitherto dedicated to agriculture. For example, the making of synthetic fuels from shale and coal requires two to four barrels of water for every barrel of fuel produced. Coal-slurry pipelines proposed to transport coal from mines in Montana and Wyoming to power plants in the South and Midwest are predicated on high water investment potentials. One such pipeline from Wyoming to Arkansas could require about 20,000 acre-feet of water per year[5] (an acre-foot is the 325,851 gallons of water that could cover an acre of land one foot deep).

Throughout the West, these varied and enormous demands for water have resulted in chronic water shortfall conditions unparalleled since the Dust Bowl days of the 1930s. In many areas of the region, the situation has become so acute that choices between food production and energy development may have to be made. Let us examine some large-scale water problem regions in the western half of the United States.

The High Plains

One of the most serious problem areas in the West is the High Plains, stretching from northern Texas to southern Nebraska. This flat, semiarid region which covers some 225,000 square miles lies over the Ogallala aquifer. Named after an Indian tribe which once roamed the High Plains, the Ogallala aquifer was formed by the receding water of the last ice age and is believed to be the largest underground reserve of fresh water on earth, containing an estimated two billion acre-feet of water trapped in sand, gravel, and silt.

The Ogallala supplies drinking water to about two million people and is the lifeblood of a rich agricultural region. High Plains cotton fields produce 25 percent of the nation's cotton, and some 40 percent of our beef cattle are produced and fattened on locally grown corn and sorghum. This high productivity is strictly dependent on irrigated agriculture.

The ancient waters trapped between a layer of impermeable slate on the bottom and an erosion-resistant cap rock on top now trickle through cotton fields in West Texas and spurt from the quarter-mile-long arms of center-pivot irrigation systems, making hundreds of circles of green corn in semiarid regions like southwestern Nebraska. Center-pivot irrigation rigs can spray 800 gallons of water per minute, or nearly 1.2 million gallons per day.

In west central Kansas the number of irrigation wells in 1950 numbered about 250; today there are over 2,850. The Ogallala currently supports irrigated agriculture on more than 11 million acres of hitherto arid land.[6] Each year farmers alone withdraw more water from the Ogallala than the entire flow of the Colorado River. Under present irrigational strategies, much of the water withdrawn for irrigation evaporates directly from High Plains fields. Sparse rainfall rarely penetrates through the impermeable cap rock to recharge the aquifer. The effects on the Ogallala aquifers have been graphic and potentially catastrophic.

In 1930, the average thickness of the area saturated with water in the Ogallala was 58 feet; today it averages less than 8 feet thick.[7] The water table is falling at a rate of 6 inches to over 3 feet per year, so that on the average the once immense Ogallala aquifer retains at best about forty years of usable life. In some places, functional depletion could occur in only a few years if consumption continues at its present pace.

In light of the wholesale overdraft of the Ogallala and other aquifers in the arid West, we should examine the once widely espoused concept known as *safe yield*. This concept, which at one time officially governed water usage from groundwater supplies, meant that aquifers should be pumped no faster than they are naturally recharged. The concept was abandoned over twenty years ago, and a new rationale which replaced it was explained by H. E. Thomas of the United States Geological Survey in his influential article, "Water and the South West—What is the Future?" in which he wrote:

Wholesale depletion (of groundwater) may be economically possible in the long view if it results in building up an economy that can afford to pay for water from a more expensive source.[8]

The general application of this viewpoint largely explains the current situation on the High Plains. The Ogallala, as a relatively cheap source of water, fueled the agricultural, industrial, and population expansion of the High Plains region from the 1950s through the present. Now that the easily exploitable water is nearly gone, we see that the underlying tenet of Thomas's argument is invalid, *because the con-*

sumption of water and energy are not mutually exclusive, but rather are inextricably linked. Exploding demophoric growth on the High Plains has led to exponential increases in both water and energy consumption, as the supply of water and the costs of energy now act together to constrain further expansion. And yet, the message that the limits of growth have been met or exceeded on the High Plains has not been fully appreciated. Further expansion, subsidized by *future* water supplies, continues.

Many experts believe that the Ogallala will never be completely drained; that its useful life is already nearly at an end. They base this argument on the fact that the expense incurred in pumping water from the Ogallala will become prohibitive in the near future.

There is ample evidence that this view is correct. Many farmers on the High Plains have already been forced to abandon irrigated agriculture due to high energy costs. Irrigated acreage is declining in five of the six states which draw water from the Ogallala with predictable results; lower crop yields, shifts from corn to less water-intensive crops like cotton and sorghum, and agricultural losses which already total in the hundreds of millions of dollars.[9] Some experts concede that corn may disappear from the High Plains by the end of the 1980s.

In Texas, the law allows for groundwater depletion allowances, much as a wildcatter exploring for petroleum is allowed for oil. But this provision has largely made a bad situation worse. Miners, developers, and big farmers have been racing each other to the bottom of the aquifer in search of quick profits. As the Ogallala is drawn further and further down, the relatively loose material comprising the aquifer is becoming compacted, so that its ability to retain water declines. Even if pumping were halted immediately, it is doubtful whether the Ogallala could ever be recharged to its original capacity.

The farms, industries, and cities of the High Plains are clearly straining the region's environmental carrying capacity dictated by water availability. The signs of both acute and chronic stress are obvious. As the High Plains region braces for the expected influx of new residents and booming energy development in the decades ahead, the future is clouded with uncertainty. A region which was once the home of now-extinct agricultural communities of Plains Indians (see chap. 5) and which was the center of the Dust Bowl of the 1930s is now coming to grips with its water economy problems. At present, three federal agencies—the U.S. Geological Survey, the Bureau of Land Reclamation, and the Department of Commerce's Economic Development Administration—are studying the impact of depletion of the Ogallala on the region's economy.[10] The region is the site of some of the most far-reaching, comprehensive regional water planning yet developed in the United States (see chap. 7). Solutions to water supply problems on so large a scale can only be arrived at when the basic causes of these problems are delimited and acted upon; long-term water usage in excess of resupply is incompatable with economic and social stability and inevitably results in a water crisis. A thirst for water which seems unquenchable must somehow be made quenchable.

The Southwestern United States

The southwestern United States is a classic example of the water supply problems which occur when too little water is coveted by too many sources of demand. Water supplies do not respect political boundaries. Severe water crises can develop when one geopolitical entity attempts to extend its growth and influence by annexing water from other areas. In the case of the Southwest, a long-term battle over the water needs of the Los Angeles Basin and other regions in northern California and Arizona has recently erupted into a full-scale confrontation[11] (see discussion of similar conflicts in historic China in chap. 5).

For many years, southern California has managed to supply water to its rapidly escalating population by importing water from other regions. More than sixty years ago, a dam and aqueduct was built in Inyo County, about 250 miles north of Los Angeles, which diverted water from the Owens River to slake the thirst of Los Angeles. Desperate farmers tried to blow up the aqueduct. A renewed conflict was touched off in 1970 when Los Angeles built a second aqueduct to the Owens Valley and began pumping water through it. These demands on Owens River water have completely desiccated a large lake which the valley once held, and dust storms frequently ravage an area hitherto covered by water. Farther north, the whole process is being repeated at Mono Lake. Water is being siphoned off and pumped some 300 miles to Los Angeles. The lake level is dropping precipitously, exposing broader expanses of bare, dry shoreline to wind erosion. History records many grand proposals to convert the Northwest into a watershed for Los Angeles and the Central Valley farmers. Rivers as far away as the Snake in Idaho and the Yellowstone in Montana have been eyed covetously. Plans have been proposed to access water from the Columbia

River, although the energy required to lift it over Oregon's mountains has stood in the way. Most of these proposals involve expenditures of tens of billions of dollars, prompting one observer to remark, "it reflects the water user's conviction that there's no need to care about conservation when there's a whole continent to go after. There's no end to people's imagination when there's a buck to be made."[12]

One of the major sources of water for southern California has been the Colorado River, which straddles the border of California and Arizona. The Colorado is an insignificant river in the nation's overall water picture; with an annual flow of 13.5 million acre-feet, it is about the same size as the Hudson River. But the Colorado is of such overriding importance to the water economy of the Southwest that barely 10 percent of its waters are allocated to Mexico. Because of a confusion of legal decisions, the seven states and Mexico through which the river flows actually have the right to withdraw more water from the Colorado than it contains. Until now, luckily, these rights have not been fully exploited. In past years, California withdrew more than its share of Colorado River water. Recent court decisions have altered this picture, prompting new concerns for residents of southern California and regions to the north.

For years, the burgeoning population and agricultural demands of central Arizona, which includes the exponentially growing communities of Tucson and Phoenix, have been devastating the meager water supplies of the state. Groundwater overdrafts have driven the water table so low that irrigation wells must now be driven over 500 feet below the surface to draw water.[13] Arizonans long angered about the excessive consumption of the Colorado by Californians were given a structural solution to their immediate problems in a Supreme Court decision in the case of *Arizona* v. *California*. The court settled in Arizona's favor, setting California's allotment of the Colorado River at 4.4 million acre-feet per year and Arizona's at 2.8 million acre-feet. Consequently, southern California, which currently imports about 5 million acre-feet of water per year from the Colorado, will have to reduce its intake in the coming years.[14]

This decision has had far-reaching ramifications for the strained water economy of the Southwest. It has spawned two major water projects which collectively threaten the fragile balance of the water economics of regions far removed from southern California and central Arizona. The Central Arizona Project and the California State Water

Project, each projected to cost billions of dollars, are schemes which seek to postpone the day of reckoning for southern California and central Arizona by extending the water annexation capacities of the respective regions. These plans, which represent classic capital-intensive, energy-intensive structural solutions of, at best, temporary usefulness will be discussed fully in chapter 7. Each proposal has been the subject of bitter controversy and vitriolic opposition because of the enormous impact they will have on regions far removed from the cities of Los Angeles, Tucson, and Phoenix.

As the once-fertile San Joaquin Valley slumps further downward each year (some 30 feet since 1930) due to excessive groundwater overdrafts, and the burgeoning population of Los Angeles continues to demand more and more of already overextended surface water supplies, the realization must inevitably come that the limits of expansion have already been exceeded. To avert wholesale water catastrophes in the arid Southwest in the years ahead may not be possible even now, for it is evident that the regional carrying capacity dictated by water availability was surpassed years ago. A commitment to a continuance of explosive demophoric growth in the Southwest is incompatible with the realities of the situation.

Other Regional Water Supply Crises

Southeastern United States

The arid West is rife with water supply crises fostered by excessive demands on overdrawn surface and groundwater reserves, but these problems are not unique to arid regions of the country. As explained in chapter 2, different groundwater formations have varying innate capacities for water recharge and total storage. For this reason, a region can develop water overdraft problems even when rainfall would seemingly be adequate for rapid water supply recharge. Further, demand for water increases exponentially as the demophoric growth of a region accelerates. Many parts of the country located in precipitation-rich regions have recorded explosive growth rates in the past decade which have fostered massive water overdrafts.

A good example of this process can be found in the southeastern portion of the United States, especially in coastal Georgia and most of Florida. This region overlies the Ocala aquifer, a large formation which was adequate to supply drinking water for millions of people for many decades. Gross overpumping of groundwater by rapidly growing communities has recently created acute and chronic water supply problems of major proportions. The general flight of people and industry to the South meant that conflicts would inevitably develop between already established agricultural water demand and new demand from immigrant people and industry. What is surprising is the speed with which these new demands for water have devastated the southeastern water economy. Heavy pumping of the Ocala aquifer has created a "cone of depression" in the water wells around most large cities in the region. One such cone, existing beneath Savannah, Georgia, is approximately 50 miles wide. Collectively, these depressions create a pressure balance which causes ocean water to be drawn into groundwater formations. Most coastal regions in the Southeast are now experiencing problems with brackish drinking water that may someday have to be remedied by pumping fresh water down into the aquifer to reestablish the pressure balance (where this water will come from has yet to be determined).

Chronic overdraft of the Ocala has created other problems. Much of the region is underlain with porous limestone which is easily dissolved by groundwater moving through it, making a honeycomb of the rock strata. When groundwater is withdrawn, the hydraulic pressure it had established in the rock formation is also removed, so that the ground slumps downward, forming sinkholes. Sinkholes have always been a part of the geology of Florida but they are increasing in frequency as the Ocala is drained.

Florida is a state only a few feet above sea level. In previous decades, the water table usually extended nearly to the ground surface, so that surface water lakes and swamps were abundant (the Everglades is a well-known example). As more water was withdrawn from groundwater reserves, the water table dropped. Diminished flow in surface seeps and rivers has resulted in potentially damaging drops in water levels in fragile marsh ecosystems. In the droughts of the past few summers, large regions of central southern Florida were devastated by grass fires in the drying marshes, further diminishing the water recharge capacity of the land as ground cover was removed.

Florida in particular is still experiencing exploding demophoric growth. Should dry conditions persist, the practice of financing today's growth with tomorrow's water reserves could have devastating effects on an overgrown population base in a rich agricultural state. In south Florida in particular, the Biscayne aquifer, which serves Miami and

Dade County, has proven to be especially prone to overdraft.[15] Florida is fifth among the continental states in total average precipitation, and recharge of groundwater is generally rapid. But because of the high yield potential of the Biscayne aquifer and the rapid rate with which it normally recharges, southeastern Florida has relied very heavily on it for water needs—up to 90 percent of all fresh water consumed in Dade County comes from groundwater. Salt water intrusion into the Biscayne aquifer was first noted in 1925. Uneven seasonal precipitation, high coastal population densities, and geological factors have rendered the Florida aquifer largely brackish in character. As the population of south Florida continues to increase, particularly due to the recent influx of immigrants, planners are scrambling to avert major, long-term water supply crises by locating more well fields inland, restricting and reallocating water consumption of off-peak use time periods, and by storing seasonally excess rain water in underground aquifers.

The Northeast

Two factors predispose the northeastern United States to water supply crises: (1) the spector of drought resulting from high altitude wind patterns, and (2) the antiquated water delivery systems in most large eastern cities which waste more water through leakage than they deliver.

In 1980 and 1981, New York City and other large cities along the eastern seaboard were locked in a serious drought. Reservoirs, which in 1980 were literally brimming with water after the spring rains, were emptied to 31 percent of capacity by the late winter of 1981.[16] In contrast, the devastating droughts of the mid-1960s had driven city reservoirs in upstate New York down to 25 percent of capacity, but that magnitude of drawdown took several years to accomplish.

New York, which had declared a water crisis emergency on 19 January 1981, faced the problem with typical aplomb. A media blitz convinced New Yorkers of the severity of the problem, and the fact that proposed conservation measures were widely adopted saved New York approximately 150 million gallons of water per day. Yet the lack of precipitation fostered continual drawdown of municipal supplies, which, as of the summer of 1981, were still critically low.

Even harder hit were smaller cities and towns in New Jersey and eastern Pennsylvania, which lacked large-scale water storage capacity. Residents in some eastern Pennsylvania communities were put on a spartan forty-gallon-per-day regime (about one-quarter of normal consumption for a family of four), enforced by fines and jail terms. The apparently cyclical nature of droughts in this region (every ten to fifteen years in recent decades) have fostered cooperative short-term water pumping arrangements between New York City and northern New Jersey, to be used under emergency water crisis conditions.[17]

The Northeast and portions of the Midwest were victims of the same drought-producing weather phenomenon: a high-pressure ridge anchored over western Canada that forced moisture-laden winds from the Pacific far north of their normal course, where they dropped rain uselessly on the ocean. A low-pressure ridge on the East Coast, meanwhile, sent Gulf Coast storms far out over the Atlantic.

The persistence of these weather patterns resulted in havoc for the northeastern water economy. Meteorologists are unsure why these patterns develop. Explanations which have been examined and rejected include sunspot activity and dust from the Mount St. Helen's eruption. Nonetheless, disconcerting evidence is accumulating which suggests that the types of high-altitude wind patterns which produced the 1980–81 drought in the Northeast and Midwest may be a harbinger of things to come. As noted in chapter 2, climate is not static, and many climatologists believe that the past several decades have been unusually wet ones in the United States.[18] Columbia climatologist Edward Cook studied tree ring patterns covering the last three centuries in the Hudson Valley and concluded that what we now consider normal weather in the Northeast has in fact been an unusually quiescent interlude. The period from 1900 to 1960 was the most stable era in the last few centuries, with little variation in annual rainfall. It was during those years that the water supply systems of the Northeast (and of course, much of the country) were planned and built. This viewpoint is shared by other climatologists, who feel that the upper altitude wind patterns of 1980–81 may be commonplace occurrences during the next few decades, thereby directly influencing the hydrologic cycle and carrying capacity of the northeastern United States.

Part of the blame for excessive drawdown of water from northeastern reservoirs can be directed at municipal water systems in these large, older cities. Because water flow is not directly metered along the routes of water conveyance systems, we do not know exactly how much water is wasted through leakage, but recent estimates place the figures between 10 and 60 percent.[19] In Boston, an ambitious and costly program to identify and repair leaky water drains has discovered that about two gallons of water are lost for every gallon delivered. The cost of replacement of essentially entire municipal water systems will run in the billions of dollars, but such action appears to be critically necessary. The loss of 100 million gallons of water per day in New York is intolerable in a city facing long-term shortages ,in the supply of fresh water. If action is deferred until water shortfalls become so acute that they threaten the viability of our older cities, the costs will undoubtedly escalate to prohibitive levels. One of the realities of water crises brought about by a contribution of drought and inefficient water delivery is that they signal an end to inexpensive water availability. As in all water crises of major proportion, the consumer of water will be asked to underwrite the technology necessary to avert catastrophic shortfalls. The merits of use planning and conservation immediately become evident to even the casual observer.

NOTES

1. J. R. Vallentyne, "Freshwater Supplies and Pollution: Effects of the Demophoric Explosion on Water and Man," in *The Environmental Future,* ed. N. Polunin (London: Macmillan and Co., 1972), pp. 181–211.

2. *Groundwater: An Overview,* CED–77–69 (Washington, D.C.: U.S. General Accounting Office, 1977), pp. 1–4.

3. Data from Economics, Statistics, and Cooperative Service, U.S. Department of Agriculture, Washington, D.C., 1979; D. Sheridan, "The Underwatered West: Overdrawn at the Well," *Environment* 23 (1981):6–33.

4. U.S. census figures for 1978.

5. K. R. Sheets, "Water: Will We Have Enough to Go Around?" U. S. News & World Report, June 29, 1981, pp. 34–37.

6. U.S. General Accounting Office, "The Taking of Private Farmland—What Should Be Done About It?" draft, April 10, 1979, p. 18.

7. Sheets, "Water," p. 35; Sheridan, "The Underwatered West," p. 9.

8. H. E. Thomas, "Water and the Southwest—What is the Future?" *U.S. Geological Circular* 469 (1962):14.

9. J. Adler et al., "The Browning of America," *Newsweek,* February 23, 1981, pp. 26–37.

10. Sheridan, "The Underwatered West," p. 9.

11. Key points in this controversy were summarized in Sheridan, "The Underwatered West," pp. 6–33; and in "The Browning of America."

12. Quote from Richard Walker in "The Browning of America."

13. Sheridan, "The Underwatered West," p. 9.

14. D. Yoder, "Aquifer Management in Dade County," *Water/Engineering and Management* 129 (1982):34–42; O. K. Buros et al., "Florida Style Water Supply and Treatment," *Water/Engineering and Management* 129, no. 4 (1982):30–33. See also J. C. Miller et al., *Ground-water Pollution Problems in the Southeastern United States*, EPA–600/3–77–012 (Washington, D.C.: Environmental Protection Agency, 1977) for a complete technical discussion of these phenomena.

15. M. Jamail et al., *Federal-State Water Relations in the American West: An Evolutionary Guide to Future Equilibrium* (Tucson: University of Arizona Press, 1978), pp. 27–30.

16. "The Browning of America," p. 29.

17. *Public Works* 113 (1982):64.

18. R. A. Bryson and T. J. Murray, *Climates of Hunger* (Madison: University of Wisconsin Press, 1977); "The Browning of America," p. 29.

19. H. Hellman, "The Day New York Runs Out of Water," *Science* 81 (May, 1981):72–75.

4 The Degradation of Freshwater Supplies

Nature never makes any blunders;
when she makes a fool she means it.

Henry Wheeler Shaw

When water supplies become degraded from human activities, that water effectively represents a net loss of potential water for human use and many agricultural applications. Some forms of water degradation are reversible; others are not. Even in cases where water can be restored, the costs are usually staggering in both monetary terms and human effort.

The degradation of water occurs in one of two ways. First, the activities of man release noxious wastes or plant nutrients into the environment and these materials become incorporated into the hydrological cycle. Secondly, man's activities alter the terrestrial or aquatic landscape in such a way as to disrupt the hydrological cycle. Both of these effects are largely preventable but have been allowed to continue through ignorance and through the mistaken notion that clean water and economic productivity are somehow incongrous. In fact, in a water-limited American society, *any* efforts directed at preserving the integrity of freshwater supplies is in the best interest of all segments of society. As we shall see, the longer degradative processes occur, the more expensive and difficult they are to rectify, if they are solvable at all.

Water Pollution

Man pollutes surface and groundwaters by adding substances to the environment which are either toxic to organisms or which facilitate the growth of organisms which we consider undesirable in our water supplies. The former case includes toxic heavy metals, radioactive wastes, natural or synthetic organic poisons, and power plant effluents which form acid rain in the atmosphere. The latter case concerns the addition of plant nutrients to water supplies from human, industrial, and agricultural wastes. The second problem has received the greatest attention in recent years because its effects on water supplies are more graphic. We will look at this second syndrome of events, a process termed *eutrophication,* first because while it represents a special case of water pollution, the general process is applicable to the dispersion and effects of any pollutant in an aquatic system. We will then consider the more dangerous cases of water pollution involving toxic wastes in surface or groundwaters.

Eutrophication and Pollution

As one travels through areas of Asia, such as much of the Peoples' Republic of China, one notes that most of the streams, rivers, ponds, and lakes are extremely productive. These surface waters have high rates of productivity because the plant life, consisting of algae and higher plants, obtain high levels of needed nutrients dissolved in the water. Because so much of contemporary life in China depends upon high plant productivity to nourish the burgeoning population of that country, nutrient loading to China's surface waters is generally encouraged.

In the United States, only an extremely small portion of total food supplies is, at present, obtained from fresh waters. Use of fresh waters for transportation, while once important (see chap. 5), is now restricted to only a few major rivers and the Great Lakes of the St. Lawrence River system. Surface waters in America are used almost entirely for freshwater supplies, utilized mostly in industry and agriculture and for disposal of man's waste products, and for aesthetic and recreational purposes. For all of these uses, it is advantageous to have the surface waters relatively pure with low content of nutrients and only low to moderate levels of plant growth. Excessive nutrient loading and increased plant productivity, the general process called *eutrophication,* results in a number of effects which Americans find undesirable for most needs.

Two aspects of eutrophication should be emphasized. First, eutrophicated surface waters are not necessarily bad—the streams and lakes are simply receiving amounts of nutrients adequate to permit plants, especially algae, to grow to their maximum levels until constrained by other factors such as light availability and temperature. If one wants the natural plant-produced organic matter or organisms that can utilize it, as in much of China, eutrophication is an advantage. If, as in America, one does not want that much plant material, because it interferes with water purification processes or results in stream or lake conditions that do not permit existence of certain desired fishes, then it is a disadvantage.

Second, eutrophication represents only a special case of pollution. Water pollution, as generally defined, is the addition of something to water which changes its natural qualities.[1] *Natural qualities* is in itself ambiguous in that the words imply some virgin state of conditions before man's activities imposed some changes. The landscape and its surface waters undergo constant alteration—natural geological processes continue to operate whether or not man is a part of the process. The point, however, is that at no time in the evolution of earth has any previous organism had the capacity to drastically alter the earth's environment. The changes man can induce are so great that his activities are now a dominant force determining the *direction* and *rates* of environmental changes, including eutrophication acceleration. Man is an integrated, driving component of nature; to discuss changes in our environment without considering human activity is simply not realistic.

Pollution is often associated with some noxious substance that man produces and releases into his environment. These substances are concentrated where they enter and may be dissipated in the environment to the point where they are dispersed and cause no noticeable change. In other cases, the substances may accumulate to haunt man when that multipurpose environment is used for some other purpose as well. The most serious pollutants are often chemical in nature, such as heavy metals, natural or synthetic organic compounds, or radioactive compounds which, when present in sufficient quantities, are toxic and cause direct harm. Other pollutants, such as natural organic compounds (e.g., plant and animal products) and natural nutrients, cause drastic changes in the environment when released in concentrated or excessive amounts. The induced changes cause conditions that make the environment, specifically surface and groundwaters, undesirable for reuse (e.g., excessive decay conditions in which decomposition of organic matter is reduced, or a shift from oxygenated to anaerobic conditions where many desired organisms cannot live).

When a lake or stream is eutrophicated with high nutrient loading, plant growth increases. In most cases the nutrients are not in themselves toxic to man.[2] Very commonly the cause is increased loading of phosphorus through man's activities. Much of the phosphorus is bound within the living and dead organisms in the water but sufficient amounts cycle very rapidly (minutes) to maintain new growth of the algae. As dying organisms settle out to the sediments, some phosphorus is carried with it and out of the upper lighted zone of photosynthetic growth. Therefore, continual phosphorus loading must take place in order to maintain high levels of plant growth.

In many streams and a large percentage (about 70 percent) of natural lakes, the most important nutrient factors limiting growth of algae and other plants are phosphorus and nitrogen. Phosphorus (P), nitrogen (N), and carbon (C) contents of typical plant tissue of aquatic algae and higher plants occur in the ratios:

1 P: 7 N: 40 C per 100 units dry weight or

1 P: 7 N: 40 C per 500 units wet weight.

If one of the three elements is limiting and all other elements are present in excess of their needs, phosphorus can generate 500 times its weight in living plants, nitrogen 71 (500:7) times, and carbon 12 (500:40) times.

Comparison of the relative amounts of different elements required for algal growth with supplies available in fresh waters illustrates the importance of phosphorus and nitrogen (table 3). Even though variations in conditions of solubility and availability may at times make very abundant elements, such as silicon and iron, and certain needed micronutrients almost unobtainable, phosphorus and secondarily nitrogen, both critical needs of the biota, are the first elements to become limiting. In other words, because phosphorus is relatively rare in the natural environment and is needed to maintain growth in expanding plant populations (e.g., algae in lakes), its demand in relation to available supplies is often much greater than for nitrogen. Similarly, the ratio of required concentrations of nitrogen to average supplies is much higher than carbon and other elements.

As phosphorus is loaded to fresh waters in supplies adequate to meet plant needs, growth increases until demand for the next commonly most required element, nitrogen, exceeds average available supplies. Then algal growth can become limited by available nitrogen.[3] The nitrogen cycle in fresh waters is complicated by the fact that a number

TABLE 3   Proportions of Essential Elements Required for Growth in Living Tissues of Freshwater Plants

Element	Average Plant Content or Requirements (in percentage)	Average Supply in Water (in percentage)	Ratio of Plant Content to Supply Available
Oxygen	80.5%	89%	1
Hydrogen	9.7	11	1
Carbon	6.5	0.0012	5,000
Silicon	1.3	0.00065	2,000
Nitrogen	0.7	0.000023	30,000
Calcium	0.4	0.0015	<1,000
Potassium	0.3	0.00023	1,300
Phosphorus	0.08	0.000001	80,000
Magnesium	0.07	0.0004	<1,000
Sulfur	0.06	0.0004	<1,000
Chlorine	0.06	0.0008	<1,000
Sodium	0.04	0.0006	<1,000
Iron	0.02	0.00007	<1,000
Boron	0.001	0.00001	<1,000
Manganese	0.0007	0.0000015	<1,000
Zinc	0.0003	0.000001	<1,000
Copper	0.0001	0.000001	<1,000
Molybdenum	0.00005	0.0000003	<1,000
Cobalt	0.000002	0.000000005	<1,000

Note: For further discussion see J. R. Vallentyne, *The Algal Bowl—Lakes and Man,* Miscellaneous Special Publications 22 (Ottawa, Ont.: Department of the Environment, 1974); and R. G. Wetzel, *Limnology* (Philadelphia: W. B. Saunders Co., 1975).

of nitrogen sources are potentially available for use by plants. Ammonium ions (NH_4^+) and nitrate ions (NO_3^-) are used most readily by the plants. Plant growth increases further and, in very productive lakes, can become limited by nitrogen supply in these forms. Certain blue-green algae that are physiologically similar to bacteria are capable of fixing gaseous nitrogen (N_2) that dissolves in the water from the atmosphere when other sources of dissolved nitrogen are available in very low quantities. These algae have a competitive advantage over other algae and most higher plants that cannot fix nitrogen. With adequate supplies of phosphorus and lowered competition from other algae, the blue-green algae often develop profusely. In need of light for this prolific growth, dense populations develop near the water surface. In addition the blue-green algae have unique mechanisms whereby they can regulate their buoyancy to assist in depth adjustments to maximize light utilization.[4] Often the blue-green algae develop in "bloom" conditions where dense populations cover lake and reservoir surfaces.

Algae growing so rapidly and densely, as all large populations, contain a portion that dies and decays. The decomposing algal organic matter can release organic compounds that humans find disagreeable or toxic when they use the water for water supply or recreation. More importantly, much of the organic matter produced in the upper, lighted portions of lakes settles to lower, dark layers of the water. As it settles, decomposition occurs. The respiration of the bacteria using this dead organic material is an oxidative process which uses oxygen dissolved in the water when it is available. As a result, oxygen is utilized in the lower depths faster than it is replaced from other sources (the atmosphere and mixing, or from plant photosynthesis and water mixing). Soon the dissolved oxygen content of the water is decreased in lower depths to concentrations where many animals, which require it, cannot live. High plant growth in the upper water layers produces more settling organic matter, increased bacterial decomposition, and increased rates of oxygen depletion.

In moderately deep lakes (more than 5–7 meters) of the temperate zones (where most lakes occur), the lake water is often thermally stratified. In the spring as the surface waters warm, the warmer water is less dense than colder water, and literally floats on top of the colder, more dense water underlying it.[5] Large amounts of energy are required to mix liquids of differing densities (e.g., cream overlying milk). Similarly in lakes, once a few degrees of difference occur between temperatures of the surface waters and those of the underlying deeper waters, even great amounts of wind on the surface are inadequate to mix completely these layers of different densities.

The water layers are not totally isolated, and complex hydrodynamics permit some exchange between the upper and lower water strata. Nonetheless, the warm, upper and the cool, lower strata are sufficiently separated that settling organic matter from plant production can decay in the lower regions and reduce or deplete the dissolved oxygen.

How effectively nutrient loading causes a lake to become more productive and less desirable for many of man's uses depends on many factors of the lake's morphometry and especially the retention time of water within the lake or reservoir.[6] If the retention time is small, as in many reservoirs that flush rapidly in comparison to many natural lakes, time can be inadequate for the biota to fully utilize high nutrient loading. In most lakes, however, the water retention times are more than adequate for the biota to respond to nutrient inputs.

There is evidence that the more stringent environmental regulations of the late 1960s and 1970s have produced marked changes in the quality of surface waters in the United States with regard to eutrophication. Nuisance blue-green algal blooms on Lake Erie, which had reached epidemic proportions by the late 1960s, have lessened significantly in recent years. Most of the central basin of Lake Erie was devoid of oxygen during the summer in the late 1960s due to massive decomposition of dead plant material in the sediments and bottom waters. As a consequence, game species of fish which required cold, oxygenated water, such as lake trout, had virtually vanished from the lake by the early 1970s.

While the pollution of Lake Erie has far from ended, an abatement of some of the more massive inputs of nutrients from large cities along the lake has occurred and the lake is gradually improving in water quality and fish species richness. Fish harvests are once again on the upswing and municipal beaches, once closed for swimming due to fecal bacterial contamination, are now open again. The enormous load of organic material and nutrients in Lake Erie sediments means that even though the lake has a relatively short water renewal time (about one year), it could take decades to return to a state approximating that of the beginning of the twentieth century. Nevertheless, progress is being made in this lake and others burdened with phosphorus and nitrogen pollution, and as long as regulations concerning the inclusion of phosphates in detergents and the release of water from municipal treatment plants remain stringent, further progress will be made.

Eutrophication is a specialized water pollution problem which has received intensive study and much attention in recent years. Every year, however, increasing amounts and varieties of other pollutants are added to our freshwater reserves. We can see that once an agent is added to an aquatic ecosystem, it rapidly becomes partitioned into many components of the system, producing myriad, poorly understood effects. The dynamic physical, chemical, and biological properties of surface and groundwater reserves dictate that, once introduced, pollutants are difficult to remove. The same properties of aquatic ecosystems also confound our a priori comprehension of the acute and long-term effects of pollutants which enter our fresh waters in ever-increasing amounts.

Problems in Water Resupply and
Water Contamination

Water supplies can be degraded and diminished by the activities of man in use of both aquatic and terrestrial environments. We have seen that the recharge of water to usable sources and its chemical composition are both affected by processes which occur on the land. The water environment and the land environment are inseparable; what occurs on the land eventually affects water. We have recently become aware that the degradation of the atmosphere also has ramifications in the hydrological cycle.

In aquatic ecology, we speak of the *watershed* as the ecosystem-level unit of organization, with the lake itself and surrounding drainage basin as communities within that ecosystem. Watershed units can be small, only a few acres in size, or they can comprise hundreds of thousands of square miles. In either case, alterations of the land environment through which water flows on its way to surface streams, rivers, and lakes, or to long-term residence in groundwater aquifers, profoundly affect water flow-through rates on the way to the ocean and the quality of water residing in each source.

Land Use Practices in Agriculture

In the 1930s much of the West and Midwest experienced conditions now referred to as the Dust Bowl. A general climatic trend toward reduced rainfall coupled with poor land use practices fostered a devastating ecological disaster which took decades to correct. A mainly invisible menace, soil erosion, forced itself into the nation's consciousness only when conditions became catastrophic. During the Dust Bowl, dry winds lifted the red, drought-stricken soil of Texas and Oklahoma into choking clouds that carried it hundreds of miles away. In just a few years, over 282 million acres of farmland were damaged.[7] Farmers abandoned their fields and the devastation grew worse. Finally, in 1935, a shocked nation executed legislation to protect the soil as Franklin Roosevelt created the U.S. Soil Conservation Service. Millions of dollars were spent instructing farmers on how to hold onto their soil, and millions more were spent in construction of terraces, windbreaks, and in the development of contour plowing, strip-cropping, and crop rotation techniques. The experiments worked. Soil erosion abated, helped along by generally increased rainfall which fostered new growth of plants to stabilize soils. By the end of World War II, the catastrophes were over and the West and Midwest again began producing bumper crops.

But soon, farmers and the government collectively decided that if a boom was good, more was better. The general availability of inexpensive water tapped from the Ogallala aquifer and from new reservoirs constructed by the Army Corps of Engineers fostered an agricultural boom which continued well to the 1970s. In their haste to maximize profits and aided by government laws which no longer paid farmers to keep tracts of land fallow, growers plowed land which had never before been planted—much of it too infertile or fragile for cultivation. The old terraces and windbreaks got in the way of gigantic modern machinery and left valuable acreage idle, so they were removed and the land seeded with grain.

By 1979, the assistant secretary of agriculture came before the House Agriculture Committee with the message that after forty years of conservation efforts, soil erosion had become worse than during the Dust Bowl days.[8] In 1979, 1.4 million acres of land were damaged by soil erosion in the ten states that comprise the Great Plains, more than double that of the previous year. Because marginal, hilly, infertile land had been planted and because farmers were no longer alternating grain crops with soil-conserving grasses, rain and snowmelt were able to strip millions of tons of soil from the land annually. Where five tons of soil lost per acre per year is accepted as the maximal safe "tolerance" limit, many agricultural regions in the West and Midwest were losing over ten tons of soil per year.

Soon it was discovered that similiar problems were widespread in the United States. Nowhere is the problem more dramatic than in the rich but fragile land of the western Tennessee counties bordering the Mississippi River. Here, cropland erosion now averages 30 to 40 tons per acre per year; some farm soil losses up to 150 tons per year have been recorded. A shift from cattle grazing to full-scale production of more profitable soybean crops has been blamed for these figures. Farmers are mortgaging their futures in the search for quick profit.

The effects of soil loss on economic returns are obvious. What is not generally realized is the effect of poor agricultural land use practices on both the supply of usable water and the degradation of available water supplies. When soil erodes from fields after a rainfall, during snow melt, or during windstorms, it does not simply move to another spot on the farm. Some does, but much of it ends up in roadside ditches and ultimately into streams, rivers, and lakes, transported by moving water through gravity flow. Agriculture thus has become the single biggest polluter of two-thirds of U.S. river basins. Eroding soil fills reservoirs with silt, impairing or ending their useful lives. Man-made reservoirs in Tennessee and in the High Plains which were designed for useful lives of a century or more will be completely filled with silt in a matter of a few decades. Similarly, navigational channels in streams and rivers must be continually dredged of silt at the cost of hundreds of millions of dollars per year.

Another process of note occurs when farm soils are eroded. During crop planting and cultivation, chemicals are added to the soil. Added nutrients and pesticides adsorb to soil particles. When the soil moves off the land, these contaminants move with it. In the past, the resulting water pollution problem mainly involved nutrients from livestock and sediment wastes, but now the input of toxic man-made chemicals is increasing to alarming proportions. Unless farm-caused water pollution is sharply curtailed by decreasing soil erosion, clean water goals mandated by Congress for this decade simply cannot be achieved.

The effects of poor land use practices on the hydrological cycle itself are less graphic but of paramount importance in water-limited America. Recall that the driving forces of the hydrological cycle are the sun and precipitation and that effective recharge of surface and groundwater supplies by incoming rainfall is dependent on that water remaining in contact with soils long enough for seepage to occur. If water is intercepted by the ground too rapidly, much of it quickly runs off or simply evaporates, so that water recharge is effectively curtailed. The latter situation is what commonly occurs on farmland where poor land use practices exist. Land denuded of vegetational groundcover or plowed in furrows which run parallel, rather than perpendicular, to ground slope simply cannot hold incoming rainfall long enough to allow for percolation, and gross runoff occurs. Downstream receiving channels accumulate vast amounts of water in a short time so that flooding often occurs. Floodwaters strip away shoreline vegetation, further exacerbating the problem, and the process becomes a vicious cycle.

No figures are available to estimate the amount of potential water recharge we are losing in the United States to these flow-through problems, but the amount is considerable and is most acute in regions already experiencing water shortages. Should climatic change further reduce intercepted precipitation, a return to Dust Bowl conditions in much of the Midwest and West is a distinct reality.

The Loss of Nonagricultural Buffer Areas

In chapter 2 we discussed the importance of natural buffer areas in regulating the hydrological cycle. We noted that wetlands, forests, and other vegetational areas are important in modulating both water recharge rates and water quality. When such buffer areas are removed, natural regulatory mechanisms which cost man nothing must be replaced artificially at considerable cost, or both the quantity and quality of water supplies suffer.

Wetlands in the United States are being drained at staggering rates for use in housing, farmland, and other development. When a wetland is drained, the watershed immediately experiences faster water flow-through rates, and erosion increases.[9] This increased loss occurs because wetlands retain water for long periods of time, facilitating percolation and moderating water runoff. Lakes and rivers downstream of a wetland receive water which has been acted upon by wetland biotic processes that remove many of the toxic pollutants and nutrients from incoming water.

A similar argument can be developed for the maintenance of undisturbed forest buffer areas.[10] Forests, with their complement of animal and plant species, process trillions of gallons of precipitation and vast tonnages of airborne and waterborne pollutants each year. The beneficial (and cost-free) effects of forests on the hydrological cycle are immensely important to man—modifying streamflow and erosion, filtering air and water, and releasing sediment-free water to surface and groundwater supplies. Large forest areas also moderate local climates, in contrast to the extremes in temperature and humidity commonly found in urban areas (see chap. 5).

Forest and other wildland soils are important filtration systems between polluted rain and human water supplies because most incoming nutrients and chemical pollutants are tightly held within the terrestrial community. Some of these contaminants include dissolved heavy metals like lead, zinc, nickel, and copper, radioactive isotopes, and persistent organic compounds like DDT. However, the water filtration capacity of natural buffer areas is not without limit. Forest and wetland vegetation and soils can absorb only a modest amount of pollutants and still function more or less normally. Eventually they come to an equilibrium with incoming pollutants and lose their storage function as a sink for potentially damaging contaminants from upstream.

These limits have been reached in many parts of the country. Heavily polluted industrial areas in Tennessee, Pennsylvania, Utah, California, and other states have been devastated by water and air pollution so that their buffering capacity has been greatly reduced or lost. We must guard against the unfounded but widely held assumption that forests and wetlands represent ultimate cures for water pollution problems.

The enormous stabilizing effects of natural buffer areas on extant water supplies can best be seen when contrasted with areas undergoing urbanization, where poor planning and careless construction techniques result in erosional rates several thousand times greater than those for a mature forest. Many of these new urban developments include small man-made ponds and lakes. In contrast to undisturbed woodland ponds, these artificial ponds located in disturbed watersheds quickly fill with silt and become eutrophicated through high nutrient loading. Pollutants from soil runoff quickly accumulate in the water and in lake sediments, so that drinking water can no longer be taken from these sources without extensive treatment. Enormous energy and capital subsidies must continually be pumped into these urbanized areas to forestall complete system breakdown. As larger and more elaborate sewage systems are built, flood control culverts constructed, and streams dredged, a huge and largely unnecessary expense is incurred by the populace through lack of understanding or application of these processes. Within a few years, a combination of decreased water percolation and faster water flow-through results in a lowered water table in the urbanized region and the cycle is complete—the region now experiences chronic water supply and degradation problems of major severity.

This syndrome of events, like most water crises, is occurring now in every part of the country. The individual, large-scale housing subdivision and its attendant environmental problems is a microcosm of the United States as a whole. In an era when both energy and water will be in short supply, developmental processes which are energy- or water-intensive or which disrupt valuable yet cost-free natural buffer areas must be seriously examined prior to implementation.

Toxic Wastes: Direct and Indirect
Water Contamination

In the past half-century human wastes and industrial effluents have so tainted our waters that by 1978, some 380 organic and heavy metal contaminants had been found in Great Lakes water.[11] The large volume of many surface and subsurface water supplies means that they are able to dilute a certain amount of toxic waste without harmful effects to human consumers of these waters. But many man-made toxic wastes become concentrated and transformed in the aquatic environment, so that the continual addition of even low levels of toxic wastes frequently renders water unfit for consumption. Further, many of these agents are persistent and may exist in water supplies for decades and even hundreds of years. We have noted that while surface waters are renewed fairly rapidly, so that contaminants can be removed by natural processes, groundwater flow and renewal is generally very slow. This slow renewal means that toxic wastes interred in groundwater supplies will stay there for hundreds of years and that removal of these contaminants becomes expensive and difficult.

The magnitude of the toxic waste problem is only now becoming apparent.[12] Few regions of the country are immune from some form of toxic waste problem and the almost daily introduction of new organic pollutants to the environment does not bode well for the future unless corrective measures are continually used.

Every year, billions of tons of solid and liquid wastes are discarded in the United States. These wastes range from relatively harmless household trash to complex materials in industrial wastes, sewage sludge, agricultural residues, mining refuse, and disease-bearing wastes. The U.S. Environmental Protection Agency has estimated that at least 57 million metric tons of the nation's total wasteload can be classified as hazardous. In hundreds of cases currently on file with U.S. government agencies, environmental damage has been recorded from the indiscriminate dumping of hazardous wastes into the terrestrial and aquatic environment.

The vast majority of the cases involve the pollution of groundwater from unproperly sited or operated landfills and surface impoundments (pits, ponds, and lagoons).[13] Still other cases document the serious effects of toxic waste contamination of surface water supplies.

Groundwater supplies in Toone and Teague, Tennessee, were contaminated, essentially irreversibly, in 1978, when organic wastes from a nearby landfill leaked into groundwater supplies. When the landfill had closed about six years earlier, the site held 350,000 drums, many of which were leaking pesticide wastes. Because the towns no longer have access to uncontaminated drinking water, they must pump water from other locations.

Groundwater in a thirty-mile-square area near Denver was contaminated from disposal of pesticide waste in unlined disposal ponds. The wastes, which date back to the 1943–57 period, were originally manufactured for the U.S. Army and a chemical company. Decontamination, if possible at all, could take several years and cost as much as $80 million.

At least fifteen hundred drums containing wastes from a metal-finishing operation were buried near Bryon, Illinois, for an unknown number of years until about 1972. Surface water, soil, and groundwater were contaminated with cyanide, heavy metals, phenols, and other toxic compounds. The damage is still being assessed and the long-range prognosis for eventual decontamination of the region is still uncertain.

About seventeen thousand hazardous waste drums littered a seven-acre site in Kentucky, subsequently known as the "Valley of the Drums." Some six thousand of these drums were full and many steadily oozed their contents onto bare ground. In 1979, an EPA survey identified about two hundred toxic organic chemicals and thirty heavy metals in soil and water samples near the dump.

No area of the country, however remote, is immune from toxic waste contamination. Because contaminants spread from point sources to large regions via regional hydrology, regions far removed from the sites of contamination frequently suffer serious effects.

Chemical contamination has forced the closing of more than six hundred groundwater wells in the New York City area over the past three years. Agents such as polychloronated biphenyls (PCBs) and other carcinogenic organic compounds such as benzene and chloroform were found in dangerous concentrations in nearly every well examined in the area. Similar problems have been found in many areas of New Jersey and in New England. As noted earlier, this region of the country is already burdened with water supply crises, so that the effective loss of major portions of groundwater for drinking could be devastating.

Corrosive liquids stored in barrels quickly move into groundwater as the barrels decompose. Once incorporated into the groundwater strata, toxins move slowly with the water flow and become dispersed, frequently contaminating large areas of groundwater. Two acute cases of this sort of contamination problem have been discovered in upstate New York and in Michigan. In New York, the region of the Love Canal has become almost infamous because of the large-scale, catastrophic groundwater pollution incurred by a leaking dump site.[14] In Michigan, nearly eight hundred groundwater and surface water contamination sites have been found. Hundreds of families around Fonda Lake in southeastern Michigan have been forced to used bottled water for three years due to road salt contamination of groundwaters. More insidious was the discovery that nearly all groundwater wells in central and western Michigan have become contaminated with PCBs, benzene, chloroform, and myriad other toxic wastes from industrial processing. Water supplies for millions of people could become unusable within a short period of time.

A federal fund has been set aside to pay for cleanup efforts involving these toxic waste dump sites and part of the costs are being assumed by the companies originally involved in the dumping. A major problem is that we really do not have cheap and effective ways to purify groundwater of toxic wastes nor can we ensure that any disposal system currently in use is capable of handling the millions of pounds of poisons produced daily in the United States.[15] In certain areas, clay-lined pits have been constructed into which wastes are dumped; it is assumed that the clay liner will be permanently impervious to leaking. Other strategies proposed include complete incineration of waste materials at high temperatures ($2500°$ F), but too few of these special incinerators are available to handle the waste load.

Some toxins are directly poisonous to man and other animals, even in minute quantities. Others, like DDT and heavy metals, can become toxic because they accumulate in the tissues of organisms and become concentrated in the food chain.[16] That is, a small amount of cadmium, for example, becomes incorporated into an algal cell, which is consumed by a small invertebrate, which is in turn consumed by a fish, which itself is consumed by man. At each step, the contaminant in question is concentrated some tenfold or more, so that the top consumer, in this case, man, receives potentially toxic doses even if a contaminant is present in only small quantities in the water. We simply do not know enough about these processes or the effects of chronic, low-level contamination on the health of humans. Until we do, we must insure that toxic waste disposal becomes a top priority item in our water management strategy.

Tragically, some of our more damaged water sources may remain unusable in our lifetimes, especially those involving groundwater contaminants of unusual persistence or acute toxicity. Those which can be restored or prevented from contamination must be protected at all costs even if these costs, which will certainly be considerable, are borne by the consumer.

Sewage treatment systems are not specifically designed to process toxic wastes. Frequently, toxic waste contamination becomes acute enough to kill bacteria important in the treatment of normal organic waste materials.

Acid Rain

Toxic wastes which leak from dump sites into ground and surface waters are directly incorporated into the hydrological cycle. But pollution can be incorporated into the flow of water in the environment even more directly: in precipitation itself. A few years ago, the term acid rain was known only to scientists. Now the scope of the acid precipitation problem in the United States and other parts of the world has become alarmingly evident.

Acid precipitation is only one special feature of general atmospheric deposition which includes three major mechanisms by which substances are transferred from the atmosphere to ecosystems: (1) adsorption and absorption of gases, (2) impaction and gravitational settling of fine aerosols and particulate material, and (3) precipitation which includes both dissolved substances and particles which are removed from the atmosphere in rain, snow, dew, fog, or frost.[17] Processes 1 and 2 are components of dry deposition and are exemplified by the settling out of materials from the Mount St. Helen's eruption. We are also becoming aware of the long-distance transfer of small aerosols swept up by winds from the world's deserts. Scientists have recently measured Sahara dust over the skies of Miami in concentrations sufficient to influence solar insolation and weather patterns.[18] As desertification processes increase the extent of the world's arid regions, including the western United States, particulate pollution of the atmosphere will undoubtedly escalate, causing indeterminate effects on local and global weather patterns and the hydrological cycle dictated by climate.[19]

The addition of materials to water from direct precipitation represents a clear and present danger to United States water supplies. By far the most serious of these problems involves the process of acid rainfall. We now know, from intensive monitoring of rainfall pH levels, that rain falling on much of the United States, Canada, and Scandinavia is highly acidic. A raindrop containing no impurities, but in equilibrium with atmospheric carbon dioxide, will attain a pH of about 5.6 or somewhat lower.[20] Because pH is a logarithmic scale, each unit change in pH represents a tenfold change in acidity. Rain falling over much of the United States, particularly in the northeastern and midwestern portions of the country, is now frequently below pH 4.5; pH values as low as 2.3 have been recorded.[21] Thus, contemporary rainfall over much of the United States is between 10 and 1,000 times more acidic than the pH 5.6 baseline.

While the mechanisms by which precipitation has become progressively more acidic over recent years are not fully understood, scientists have established that the primary source of hydrogen ions that cause the phenomenon of acid rain are the strong mineral acids, sulfuric and nitric acid, present in atmospheric water vapor.[22] These acids result largely from chemical reactions between atmospheric water and sulfur and nitrogen oxides released into the atmosphere as a consequence of fossil fuel combustion, especially coal and oil.[23]

Acid rainfall causes innumerable changes in both terrestrial and aquatic ecosystems.[24] Many terrestrial plants are extremely sensitive to rainfall pH and are directly damaged by acid rain. Acid rainfall affects the ion composition of terrestrial soils through leaching of nutrients and mobilization of heavy metals. Terrestrial soils in forested areas are less sensitive to low levels of acidic precipitation because of their natural buffering capacities. There is no question that continued influx of acidic precipitation will soon damage terrestrial systems, but even now, more fragile lake systems are being damaged by pollution from the sky.

As noted in chapter 2, surface waters differ in their relative chemical buffering capacities. The buffering capacity can be roughly defined as the ability of a given body of water to resist changes in pH when acids or bases are added. This capacity is of fundamental importance because many aquatic organisms cannot tolerate wide changes in water pH and because both geological and chemical changes and reactions in both aquatic systems and their surrounding terrestrial watersheds are dictated by ambient pH levels.

Lakes and other bodies of water situated in geological regions comprised of relatively hard igneous rock are generally poorly buffered. As might be expected, these lakes suffer most acutely from even small influxes of hydrogen ions from incoming precipitation. Most of the lakes in the northeastern United States and southeastern Canada fall under this classification. In the Adirondacks, hundreds of lakes are now showing signs of acute and chronic acidification. In just the last few years, many lakes of the entire lake district in upstate New York have largely been depleted of game fish because acidic lake waters interfere with fish reproductive cycles and change the composition of the algal communities which form the basis of the aquatic food chain. In addition, acidic precipitation falling on terrrestrial watersheds has mobilized heavy metals from the parent rock and soils; aluminum toxicity in the receiving basins of these watersheds has contributed to depleting many lakes of nearly all macroscopic animal life.

While the Northeast is, by definition, inordinately prone to acidic perturbation, the same processes are occurring in other regions, notably Minnesota, Wisconsin, Michigan, Florida, and parts of the Pacific Northwest. Regions far removed from industrial activity become afflicted with acid rainfall problems because wind currents carry nitrogen and sulfur oxides far from the sites of origin, depositing enhanced concentrations of acid in previously pristine areas.

Long-distance transport of airborne contaminants has become more serious in recent years because of the introduction of tall stacks to power plants and smelters, which result in lowered local emissions of pollutants, but which simultaneously increase the geographical area downwind affected by effluent gases and particulates. Even environmental legislation aimed at decreasing stack emissions has had its drawbacks. Scrubbers, mounted on tall stacks at considerable expense, remove alkaline particulate material from stack emissions, which simultaneously increases the acidic character of residual pollutants reaching the atmosphere and thereby the acidity of downwind precipitation.[25]

The precise cause and effect relationships between acid precipitation and pollution sources are still being intensely debated and investigated.[26] The overwhelming consensus of scientific opinion, however, relates the current 30 to 35 million tons of sulfur and nitric oxides emitted to the atmosphere each year from combustion of fossil fuels in North America to much of the increased acidity of precipitation and fresh waters in sensitive geographical areas.

As the United States' energy demands foster increased use of coal in power generation, the prospects for abatement of acid rain become more uncertain but at the same time more critical. As is the case in toxic waste disposal, we can ill afford to espouse the attitude, "out of sight, out of mind," when it comes to atmospheric pollution. To abdicate responsibility in the name of cost-effectiveness and short-term profit is to invite long-term damage and far greater costs, human and economic, in the future.

NOTES

1. Many definitions exist but all focus on this central concept. See for example H.B.N. Hynes, *The Biology of Polluted Waters* (Liverpool: Liverpool University Press, 1960).

2. Concentrations of common nutrients, such as nitrate, can be increased to levels where they can become toxic. For example, above about 10 mg per liter, nitrate could cause harm to infants. In most streams and lakes, such levels of nitrate are not normally reached.

3. N. G. Carr and B. A. Whitton, eds., *The Biology of Blue-green Algae* (Berkeley: University of California Press, 1973); and G. E. Fogg et al., *The Blue-green Algae* (New York: Academic Press, 1973).

4. R. G. Wetzel, *Limnology* (Philadelphia: W. B. Saunders Co., 1975).

5. Ibid.

6. Ibid.

7. J. Risser, "A Renewed Threat of Soil Erosion: It's Worse Than the Dust Bowl," *Smithsonian* 11, no. 12 (1981):120–30.

8. Ibid.

9. R. E. Good, D. F. Whigham, and R. L. Simpson, eds., *Freshwater Wetlands: Ecological Processes and Management Potential* (New York: Academic Press, 1978); P. E. Greeson, J. R. Clark, and J. E. Clark, eds., *Wetland Functions and Values: The State of Our Understanding* (Minneapolis: American Water Resources Association, 1979); B. Gopal, et al., eds., *Wetlands: Ecology and Management* (Jaipur, India: National Institute of Ecology and International Scientific Publications, 1982).

10. F. H. Bormann and G. E. Likens, "The Fresh Air–Clean Water Exchange," *Natural History* 86, no. 9 (1977):63–71.

11. The actual values increase almost daily as more sophisticated instrumentation is used to analyze lake water. Each year, literally hundreds of new synthetic organic compounds are developed. A central maxim in ecology is that nothing ever goes away in the environment, it only changes form. The ultimate fate of many organic contaminants is to move irrevocably into water supplies.

12. J. C. Fine, "Toxic Waste Dangers," *Water Spectrum,* Winter, 1981, pp. 24–30. U.S. Environmental Protection Agency, *Everbody's Problem: Haz-*

ardous Waste, SW–826 (Washington, D.C.: Government Printing Office, 1980). p. 1.

13. Fine, "Toxic Waste Dangers," pp. 1–2.

14. Ibid.

15. Ibid., pp. 26–30. The entire concept of toxic waste disposal in landfills is fraught with controversy. Many scientists and engineers feel that so-called safe dump sites, that is, those isolated from groundwater and surface water seepage, are not really safe at all, even when clay-lined pits are used. The problem is that many wastes have toxic lives of several thousands of years, (i.e., radioactive wastes and some persistent organic wastes) and no method yet devised can insure perpetual care of these materials. In any case, the costs of safe interment will be high ($50 to $2,000 per cubic yard of waste) and costs are rising precipitously: cf. A. W. Breidenbach, P. B. Lederman, and R. B. Pojasek, "Disappointment of the Seventies, Expectations of the Eighties," *Journal of Water Pollution Control Federation* 53, no. 2 (1981):152–54.

16. C. H. Mortimer, "Props and Actors on a Massive Stage," *Natural History* 87, no. 7 (1977):51–58.

17. E. B. Cowling, "A Status Report on Acid Precipitation and Its Ecological Consequences as of December 1980," Paper delivered to participants of the Workshop on Ecological Effects of Acid Precipitation, March 4–6, 1981, Atlanta, Georgia, p.2

18. J. M. Prospero, "Dust from the Sahara," *Natural History* 88, no. 5 (1978):55–61.

19. D. Sheridan, "The Underwatered West: Overdrawn at the Well," *Environment* 23, no. 2 (1981):6–33.

20. Cowling, "Status Report," p. 2. For a number of chemical reasons related to natural atmospheric compounds and particles, the pH of rainwater is often lower than pH 5.6 (R. Sequeira, "Acid Rain: An Assessment Based on Acid-Base Considerations," *Journal of the Air Pollution Control Association* 32 [1982]:241–45). Acid precipitation is often arbitrarily defined as precipitation with a pH of less than 5.6. Although this definition is not very realistic, it does serve as a general arbitrary basal point for comparisons.

21. J. A. Lynch and E. S. Corbett, "Acid Precipitation—A Threat to Aquatic Ecosystems," *Fisheries* 5, no. 3 (1980):8–12.

22. Cowling, "Status Report," pp. 1–21; R. Patrick et al., "Acid Lakes from Natural Anthropogenic Causes," *Science* 211 (1981):446–48.

23. Cowling, "Status Report," pp. 1–3; Patrick, "Acid Lakes," p. 446.

24. Bormann and Likens, "Fresh Air–Clean Water," pp. 63–71; Lynch and Corbett, "Acid Precipitation," pp. 8–10; Cowling, "Status Report," pp. 1–21; N. R. Glass et al., "Effects of Acid Precipitation," *Environmental Science and Technology* 16 (1982):162A–169A.

25. Cowling, "Status Report," p. 2.

26. Electric Power Research Institute, *Proceedings: Ecological Effects of Acid Precipitation,* EA-2273 (Palo Alto, Calif.: Electric Power Research Institute, 1982); Comptroller General of the United States, *The Debate Over Acid Precipitation: Opposing Views, Status of Research,* EMD–81–131 (Washing-

ton, D.C.: U.S. General Accounting Office, 1981); G. Morling, "Effects of Acidification on Some Lakes in Western Sweden," *Vatten* 1(1981):25–38; L. S. Evans et al., "Acidic Precipitation: Considerations for an Air Quality Standard," *Water, Air, and Soil Pollution* 16(1981):469–509; L. S. Evans, "Biological Effects of Acidity in Precipitation on Vegetation: A Review," *Environmental and Experimental Botany* 22(1982):155–69; D. W. Johnson et al., "The Effects of Acid Rain on Forest Nutrient Status," *Water Resources Research* 18(1982):449–61; F. M. D'Itri, ed., "Acid Precipitation: Effects on Ecological Systems" (Ann Arbor, Mich.: Ann Arbor Science, 1982).

5 Human Populations and Water Crises: A Historical Perspective

What a piece of work is man! How noble in reason!
How infinite in faculty! . . . In action how like an
angel! In apprehension how like a god!

Shakespeare

Man is Nature's sole mistake.

William Gilbert

We have met the enemy and he is us.

Pogo

Neither physically strong nor fleet of foot, we have been successful as a species primarily because our technological culture enables us to alter our environment to suit our needs. However, the same societal forces which fostered the ascent of man have also precipitated countless environmental crises and cultural decline.

Shakespeare notwithstanding, Mankind is neither godlike nor omniscient. Simply stated, man is an animal, and like all organisms, his reproductive success is constrained by physical and biological processes. Chief among these constraints is the size of an exploitable but limited resource base.

Water resource crises are not new to late-twentieth-century America. Human cultures throughout history seem prone to expanding beyond the limits dictated by water availability. The point of this historical perspective is that it illustrates the societal problems which develop when these limits are not appreciated. Almost all of our contemporary water supply and water degradation crises have parallels in history. We can learn from the mistakes of these other cultures as we repeat the same deadly pattern. To fully appreciate the scope of water crises in contemporary America, we also need to examine the historical development of our attitude about water.

The United States is a society in adolescence, with the technological power to fundamentally alter its physical world, but lacking in experienced wisdom to direct this power. The explosive technological growth which made our societal childhood so successful threatens to prevent our transition into stable maturity in what will certainly be a water-limited state. We continue our present course at our peril. The full implications of uncontrolled, explosive growth and its effects on our finite water resources must be appreciated and acted upon in a reasoned, even ruthless manner.

A Legacy of Water Resource Crises

There is no doubt that at the present time, all human societies, advanced and developing, are facing one aspect or another of an environmental crisis of major proportions. In the United States, water and energy are both in short supply and competition for these resources is keen. In other countries, critical mineral resources may be scarce, such as is the case in Japan and Western Europe. In underdeveloped nations, particularly in drought-stricken Africa, many peoples struggle with the ever-present specter of famine.

To be sure, at least some of the manifestations of these crises are brought about by circumstances beyond the direct control of man, such as global climatic change. However, the roots can be traced to one cause: too many people are competing for the same scarce resources within a geographical area possessing finite resources.

Environmental crises brought about by scarcity in one or more limiting resources are not new to the last years of the twentieth century, but have, in their present form, been with us since man first banded together in concentrated settlements. Traditionally, industrial civilizations like our own believe as an article of faith that most such crises belong in the past. We believe that any resource limitation, even those involving fresh water, can be overcome by the application of an appropriate technological fix. Unfortunately, this widely held belief is erroneous. History tells us that technological cures for water problems typically result in new problems for succeeding generations to solve.[1] Furthermore, water shortfalls can result from climatic change beyond man's control and no technology can extract water which is not there.

Why do human cultures seem predisposed to water resource crises? What is the typical societal response to water demand shortfalls?

Societies typically implement three possible strategies to acquire more water when their own supply has diminished. The first strategy is to employ technological solutions to increase the extraction of water from hard-to-get-at sources. These solutions can be as primitive as oxen-driven well pumps or as sophisticated as massive irrigation projects that carry water from distant places to sites of need. Such stepping-up of extractive capacity inevitably results in greater energy expenditures and environmental degradation and in further damage to limited water supplies.

Yet more environmental degradation occurs, however, when a society opts for the second possible strategy. The present technology is maintained and the populace expands into another as yet unexploited region. We in the United States used this "frontier approach" (and still do) as people moved ever westward into previously unexploited territory.

People also alleviate resource shortfalls by taking them from other people. Societies have always spent huge sums of money to prevent such threats. While war is theoretically forbidden internationally, it was until recently organized as a legitimate procedure. Thus the western hemisphere came to be populated by Europeans and in the same manner California was added to the United States. Witnessing the clamor for Middle East oil, we see that such strategies are far from dead.

All of these strategies—technological change, migration, and annexation—become necessary when a human population exceeds a given environment's carrying capacity and still wishes to maintain an evolved standard of living. Ecologists use the term *carrying capacity* to denote the maximum population size a given environment and its resource base can support. Neither human nor bacterial populations can long increase their numbers beyond this maximum level. Inevitably, demand for limiting resources must decrease. In human populations, this decrease in demand has been accomplished by such repugnant means as war, famine, plague, and mass exodus.

We humans often overshoot our environmental carrying capacity. When living conditions are good, humans tend to reproduce rapidly; slight changes in societal food production or in the supply of limited resources such as water result in a new, lower carrying capacity, and hard times follow for the overgrown population. Other factors predispose humans to excessive population. We have a nine-month gestation period; additionally, full resource needs do not develop until after adolescence. In many societies, including our own, much of the population is below this age, so additional demands are delayed and will be imposed on resources even without further increases in numbers. We can easily generate famine or water scarcity, for instance, where our populations have inadvertently increased to the point where, when they mature, they will exceed the carrying capacity for these resources.[2]

Because water is consumed by people in so many ways and because it supports food production and technology, it is and has always been the fundamental limiting resource constraining the growth of human societies, and the first resource controlled by man during his cultural evolution. As we view the long history of human environmental crises and the misery they caused, we see that water shortfalls, more frequently than not, were fundmental components of these crises.

Water Resource Crises in Other Cultures

Water resources can be profoundly influenced by forces beyond man's direct control. One of the most important of these forces is climatic change. We tend to view climate as fixed over short periods of time such as several hundred years or several decades. The truth is that climate fluctuates markedly even within periods of decades. These fluctuations, which influence both the amount and distribution of precipitation, the driving force of the hydrological cycle (see chap. 2), alter the carrying capacity of a given environment with great speed. A culture closely tied to a particular climate then finds itself in jeopardy, because its population structure is geared to existing water supplies which have suddenly been reduced or cease to exist. Technological application can temporarily alleviate water supply or quality shortfalls. But no society can long endure when the absolute supply of water received is greatly diminished, and such cultures are plunged into chaos.

The Mill Creek People

Stretching across the Great Plains from Iowa to Colorado, covered by the dust of centuries, lie the remnants of a thousand small villages. Once they teemed with life—for generations the cycle of seasons and the cycle of life went on, summer cultivation alternating with winter hunting. In the sixteenth century, when Coronado traversed the plains in search of the cities of gold, he found no cities and very few agricultural villages.[3] When the westward expansion of American commenced in the nineteenth century, no agricultural societies at all were found on the plains. Where had all the farmers gone and why had they abandoned their villages?

We have learned much about these puzzling questions in the last several years from archaeological work conducted on the Mill Creek People of northwestern Iowa.[4] From excavations of their settlements, we know that these people were corn-growers and that for generations ample rain had resulted in bountiful harvests. From about A.D. 900 to A.D. 1200, their numbers and villages increased and soon similar agricultural societies occurred across the plains. Yet, about A.D. 1200, these societies began declining and by A.D. 1400, they had largely disappeared. Climatologists have recently proposed a plausible scenario for the demise of Plains agricultural societies.

Northwestern Iowa, like much of the Great Plains, is a borderland; specifically this area is an *ecotone,* or transition zone between a more arid short-grass region to the west and a wetter, tall-grass prairie to the east. An ecotone, by definition, is an area sensitive to even small climatic changes. We know that contemporary northwestern Iowa receives about 25 inches of precipitation per year. Generally, this amount of rain produces good corn and soybean harvests, but the rainfall is not always enough to compensate for hot summer winds. Even present-day agriculture is frequently water-limited.

By piecing together archaeological and climatological data, scientists have established that the climate of the Great Plains changed drastically around A.D. 1200, resulting in a great drought which lasted approximately two hundred years. We now believe that this drought devastated the Plains agricultural societies. Previous centuries of bounty had resulted in exponential population growth among these peoples. When the climate changed, their culture was quickly thrust into a situation in which their numbers and water needs far exceeded the reduced carrying capacity of their environment. Famine and mass emmigration resulted and settlements had to be abandoned for a nomadic, less centralized life-style. The end came just before the rains returned again around A.D. 1400 but by then the damage had been done.

The Great Plains, where much of our food is grown and where increasingly large industrial complexes are located, remains an ecotone. How would we, the exponentially expanding society of the twentieth century, have fared under similar circumstances of major climatic change?

Ancient China

Chinese environmental crises, during a period from about the eighth century through the third century B.C., can be described in rather similar terms as our own contemporary problems.[5] No census records exist from that early period, but there are indisputable signs of a rapidly growing population and of social changes associated with the emergence of middle-class business communities. New cities were built in great numbers and a multistate power structure began to develop.

Population growth, economic development, and the increasing need for military preparedness resulted in intense competition for increasingly scarce resources and often erupted in war, creating a series of famines. By the fourth century B.C., famine in many areas had reached crisis proportions. These crisis conditions repeatedly occurred and were not stemmed until widespread social, economic, and political adjustments occurred in the Chinese world.

During lulls between wars, state bureaucracies gave rulers the organizational capacity of channeling money into major irrigation projects. In the late sixth and early fifth centuries B.C., much irrigation and transport canal construction occurred. In addition to construction of several major canals, "there were literally millions of smaller canals which led off from the larger ones at numerous points along their courses and were employed to irrigate an increasingly large area of land."[6] These canals and increased adoption of new techniques in agriculture, such as the development of bronze and iron tools and the implementation of fallowing and manuring techniques, brought much wealth to the areas in which they were used, and temporarily increased the standard of living.

None of these technological developments, however, proved sufficient to remedy permanently the difficulties of the Chinese states. New problems appeared and underlying problems remained. More iron had to be smelted, resulting in increased demand for wood to make charcoal. Deforestation resulted in widespread erosion and degradation of water supplies. The population grew enormously, quickly absorbing any surpluses and further accelerating demands on precious resources.

Most serious of all was the increased use of these newfound and ephemeral surpluses to fuel still-existing rivalries between states for their share of power and resources. Renewed warfare again plunged China into a series of famines and a new round of environmental crises, made more serious this time by the highly degraded nature of their water supplies and the demand of the expanded population for food and water.

The ecological crisis conditions which persisted after the fourth century B.C. altered the balance of power in China. The state of Ch'in, one of China's more remote and underdeveloped provinces before the onset of acute environmental difficulties, took advantage of their relatively high resource potential and concentrated these resources on internal development. Instead of putting human and economic resources into the central Chinese battleground, Ch'in acquired vast new territories, turning them into new resource bases. Immigrants came into these underdeveloped lands and put these areas into production. Ch'in officials imposed strict regimes which encouraged agricultural production and invested large sums of money in the construction of two immense irrigation systems which made even more land available for settlement. From this newfound wealth Ch'in raised China's most powerful army, and in the 230s and 220s B.C., used its forces to conquer and unify all states.

The Ch'in unification finally brought a temporary end to China's ecological crisis. Although it lasted but a dozen years, its successor state, the former Han Dynasty, built a regime which lasted two hundred years, and bequeathed its traditions to other dynasties which succeeded it for two thousand years.

The unification of China ended the threat of war and allowed more resources to be used for production of food. However, these accomplishments were garnered only through severe losses in personal freedom among the Chinese people. As the Chinese outgrew their technological advances, creating increasingly severe environmental problems, particularly in water availability for human consumption and agricultural use, the only ultimate solution came with rigid governmental control over individual rights. We, too, have developed one technological innovation after another to raise sagging productivity and extract increasingly depleted water resources from the environment. We in contemporary America must evaluate if, as we approach the limits of technological solutions, individual rights can be maintained within the growth of government controls brought on by immense social and environmental pressures.

Medieval Europe

The European experience is valuable because it is from this background that historical and contemporary American attitudes about water developed. In mid-fourteenth-century Europe, one out of every four persons perished within a span of three years and the total number of dead may have surpassed twice the number killed in Europe during World War II.[7] Historians are still trying to assess the impact of the Black Plague on European society and its institutions. One point is clear, however. The Black Death was not an isolated disaster, for the plague was but one of a series of events precipitated by environmental crises, especially those involving water.

While no modern historian would ascribe to the then popular theory that the plague was a divine punishment on Europeans caused at least partially by the sins which the Europeans committed against their natural environment during the twelfth and thirteenth centuries, they do insist that ecological crises were root causes of plague-induced disasters. Mortality rates were high, because the lower-class population was chronically undernourished at the time. Widespread famine occurred largely because food production was drastically reduced by the ravishing of the environment during the two preceding centuries.

The fourteenth century has been viewed as a classic example of Malthusian economics at work.[8] Populations pressed against resources while no technological breakthrough permitted better resource acquisition or utilization. Famines, riots, and wars became more frequent as human beings struggled for larger slices of a diminishing pie until nature struck in the form of a plague, reducing population and rapidly restoring equilibrium. Clearly, the crises of the fourteenth century were rooted in the inordinate expansion of the preceding epoch.

In the year 1050, Europe was still largely covered by forests with only isolated islands of human habitation. Although the populations around individual villages were quite dense, the forests were seen as the enemy of man, the abode of demons and hobgoblins, and ill suited for human habitation. In contrast, by 1300 there were villages everywhere and forests almost nowhere.

The great deforestation of the Middle Ages began harmlessly enough. At first, only lands adjacent to villages were cleared. As the population swelled, more and more marginally productive lands were cleared for agriculture and negative effects soon began to mount. By 1300, there is evidence that large river systems and their accompanying watersheds were being severely affected by poor land use practices. Grain crops along the upper Rhine River were frequently destroyed in the fertile floodplain due to excessive flooding caused by rapid runoff from denuded slopes.

The great clearings of the twelfth and thirteenth centuries were necessitated by spectacular population increases. Experts agree that the population of Europe doubled and perhaps tripled during this era. New agricultural techniques and expansion fostered two centuries of population growth as food became more available. The urbanization of Europe produced literally thousands of towns with between five and ten thousand inhabitants, often in places where no settlements had been before. Many cities grew to house over one hundred thousand inhabitants. Increasingly, fewer and fewer people had to support the food requirements of increasing numbers of urban dwellers. The pressures on finite natural resources became enormous, and soon there was little virgin, fertile land left to exploit.

The unprecedented growth of European population, urbanization, and commerce resulted in new attitudes about nature. Men no longer considered themselves victims of nature, but rather her master. The subjugation of the European environment provided the basis for exponential growth. Shortly after 1300, things began to go wrong.

Two centuries of explosive expansion had been purchased on credit using Europe's diminished resource base as collateral. In the fourteenth century, nature foreclosed. Water resources, degraded by human wastes in the cities and by erosion in the countryside, could sustain no further growth. The human carrying capacity of the European countryside had been exceeded.

Disease spread by contaminated water swept through urban areas. Famine resulted when degraded farmlands ceased to produce surpluses needed to feed the urban masses. The populace, weakened by hunger and debilitated by infectious disease, was decimated by the Black Plague, a disease for which Europeans had no natural immunity. While plague was the outward manifestation of crisis, the root cause was the disruption of the hydrological cycle in Europe and the degradation of its extant water supplies.

In a manner similar to the Mill Creek People, Europeans also felt the effects of worldwide climatic changes which commenced around 1300. As the American Great Plains was becoming drier, Europe became increasingly cool and wet. This wet, cool weather deteriorated grain crops both before and after harvest.

As a result of rapid climatic change, famine became common during the fourteenth century. The most serious of these recurring famines illustrates how rapidly climatic change can induce population stress. The summer of 1314 had been an unusually wet year, and yields were low all over Europe. When abnormal rainfall continued in 1315, acute crisis loomed on the horizon. By the spring of 1316, stored grain reserves had been exhausted and mass starvation hung over the land. Within two years, Europe was plunged into mass chaos. Records show that this cycle recurred at approximately decade intervals throughout the rest of the century. The price of grain increased three to fivefold during the first years of famine. In some Flemish towns, which had long been dependent on imported grain, one person in ten died during the years 1315–17.

The wet weather also affected grain after it was harvested. During damp, cool weather, a strange madness accompanying a deadly illness periodically reached epidemic proportions in Western Europe.[9] Whole villages would suffer convulsions, hallucinations, gangrenous rotting of the extremities, and often death. Because the blackened, gangrenous hands and feet looked as if they had been burned, the disease was likened to fire; it was often called St. Anthony's fire, named after a monastic order of the Hospital Brothers of St. Anthony which was founded to care for the victims of the disease.

Late in the sixteenth century, though the disease was then uncommon, the poison which wrought such havoc was identified. It was contained in kernels of rye affected with ergot blight—the fungus now known as *Claviceps purpurea*. The blighted kernels are blackened and enlarged, and only a few in a sack of flour are enough to affect those who eat bread made from it. This fungus thrives in blighted grain stored in wet, cool weather and its widespread occurrence during the thirteenth century further accelerated population suffering.

We can speculate that the suffering of the thirteenth century might not have occurred at all if climatic changes had not occurred. Nevertheless, the evidence is overwhelming that the enormous growth of European society during the preceeding two centuries and the accompanying degradation of the European landscape, particularly of its water resources, were the prime root causes of the decline of European society.

Societal attitudes about nature which fostered environmental crises in medieval Europe have, for better or worse, become a part of American culture as well. The aggressive, uncontrolled exploitation of resources characteristic of twelfth- and thirteenth-century Europe was echoed later as Europeans developed and exploited the American continent. In our efforts to develop adequate responses to our own water resource problems, we should not neglect the experience, perhaps even the wisdom, accumulated by the centuries-long European situation.

Victorian London and the Great Stink of 1858

The water crises faced by Londoners in the nineteenth century have many parallels with our own situation in the United States. Since the English system of government and social mores are so similar to our own, it is instructive to note how Victorian London dealt with the myriad water crises of its day.

The Industrial Revolution which developed in England during the latter part of the eighteenth century and the nineteenth century produced an enormous influx of people into large industrial cities. The water problems caused in urban areas by this demographic shift and resultant societal responses have interesting implications for our present situation.

A city is a place characterized by a permanent heat island, differentiated from the surrounding countryside not only in terms of ambient temperature but also in terms of humidity and, most importantly, water storage and recharge capacity. Permanent heat island effects seem to exist in human settlements with populations in excess of around ten thousand.[10] The net effect of urbanization is that the environmental and geopolitical influence of an urban area soon extends far beyond political boundaries.

By definition, urban areas are ecologically unstable. There are two primary causes of urban instability. First, the physical structures of the city destroy the habitats of many species (while creating other habitats, to be sure). Second, the overburdened biomass of the urban area requires external inputs of food and water while retaining organic waste within the system. Because of these factors, urban ecosystems lack many of the homeostatic controls built into stable, natural systems. For this reason, urban systems are easily disturbed, and their resilience after perturbation is dependent on sociocultural as well as natural factors.

The most crucial urban management problems have historically been the elimination of organic waste and the supply of clean drinking water.

Water problems in London can be traced back to late medieval times.[11] In the early 1370s and again in the 1420s, the municipal Letter Books show a clustering of complaints about sewage overloads, doubtless reflecting population growth. Underlying sewage overcharging was the phenomenal expansion of the city's physical plant, which quickly absorbed natural streams, important waste removal sites, and reduced water recharge through percolation.

The city had built a reservoir at Tyburn in the mid-thirteenth century, and water was pumped into the city through a conduit. The reservoir itself was created in response to water lost to the city through pollution of the Thames River and the despoiling of wells.

In contrast, London had no man-made sewer system until after the fire of 1666. This system grew throughout the eighteenth century, reaching a level of exponential growth between 1827 and 1851 which brought the total length of sewers to forty-nine miles.

Nonetheless, as Victorian London's societal organization and technological capacities increased, so too had the magnitude of its water problems. It became increasingly evident that piecemeal implementation of technological fixes was simply creating new and even worse problems than had occurred before.

Victorian London during the 1850s typified an unfortunate but universal characteristic of human society: unless a problem is forcibly and graphically thrust upon it, the problem is ignored. London's "Great Stink" of 1858 is a perfect example in microcosm of the response syndrome all human societies tend to employ to deal with acute and inescapable environmental crises.

Edwin Chadwick, the leader of the public health movement, had, for some twenty years prior to the Great Stink, lobbied for a metropolitan approach to drainage as well as other sanitary problems. For political reasons, he was effectively blocked. Parliament was reticent to deal with these matters, since non-Londoners were unwilling to commit their constituent's tax monies for London's problems, and various boroughs of the city resisted attempts to disperse their power.

His drive for metropolitan drainage stymied, Chadwick turned to house drainage, promoting the installation of water closets in new houses and the replacements of cesspools by water closets in old ones. By the end of 1853, about one-tenth of the homes in London, or about twenty-seven thousand, were drained by pipes. This method effectively reduced the pollution of individual wells and small streams within London. However, since the water closets ultimately had to drain into the Thames River, Chadwick's plan contributed to overloading the Thames with raw sewage, bringing about intense anaerobic decomposition and the Great Stink.

The important point is that Chadwick's plan, while getting rid of one water crisis, promptly produced another of far greater dimensions. The central theme of Chadwick's project was that direct pollution of a relatively large, flowing body of water like the Thames, while potentially disgusting to the senses, was not in itself a danger to public health. In this, he was supported by chemists, including some of Britain's most eminent scientists.

In report after report, and in testimony before parliamentary commissions, eminent chemists gave the river a clean bill of health, contrary to medical opinions. The chemists' findings stressed the Thames's great capacity for self-purification, whereby impurities were leached out by filtration and aeration in the natural course of the river's flow, so that except in extraordinary circumstances, drinking water could be obtained "entirely free from suspended solid matter, or mechanical impurities." In other words, the contamination was more aesthetic than lethal and was largely removed by natural means.

Population pressures had long since forced Londoners to use water from the Thames and other contaminated sources for drinking. The reason chemists could make such health assertions was largely due to the prevailing view on microbial pathogenicity in water.

The notion that "animacules" in water were harmless was the opinion of the great English chemist Justus Liebig. Others were not so sure. In cross-examination by a parliamentary commission, a microbiologist, A. H. Hassall, was asked for his opinion about Liebig's assertion that "it is quite certain that water containing living infusoria becomes a source of oxygen gas when exposed to the action of light; it is also certain that as soon as these animals can be detected in the water, the latter ceases to be injurious to plants and animals." Hassall rejected this statement entirely. He and most physicians knew otherwise. Cholera had recently been unequivocally linked to human sewage. Hassall felt that the presence of large numbers of infusoria in water was in itself a clear indication of impurity. He had found the largest numbers of microbes in the Thames in the vicinity of bridges, where the main sewers discharged.

The chemists believed that disease was caused by "miasma" emitted by decaying organic matter. The putrefaction of the Thames, they argued, could be fully taken care of (and hence disease eliminated) by the self-purifying properties of the river.

The gap between Hassall's opinion and that of the chemists could not be bridged. Consequently, matters continued as they had until June of 1858, when the problem ceased to be academic. The Thames had for many years reeked in the summertime, but during the Great Stink of 1858, the river became so odious as to cast a pall over the entire city. The *Lancet* rejoiced: "Fortunately, the hideous—the truly horrible, state of the River Thames is at last, not only attracting universal attention, but it is exciting a feeling of public indignation which will not be easily repressed" (Glick 1980, p. 133). The citizenry took great joy in the fact that members of Parliament had to exit their august chambers with handkerchief to nose.

The Stink produced a flurry of activity and general uncertainty as to what action really ought to be taken. The windows of committee rooms at Parliament were opened and covered with canvas soaked in chloride of lime to deodorize and purify the air. Other ludicrousness prevailed. Gurney, a Parliament staffer and self-taught engineer, proposed to run pipes from the sewers of London to direct the sewer gases into high towers, which, when ignited, would rid the city of noxious gases, and, at the same time, provide a pleasant, blue nocturnal illumination.

The solution finally adopted was one recommended by chemists and engineers. Tons of chalk lime, chloride of lime, and carbonic acid were dumped into the river to purify it. Meanwhile, of course, the sewers continued to load directly into the Thames. Even the *Lancet* acknowledged that the only real solution was to totally intercept London's raw sewage and to treat it.

Total interception was, of course, a political problem. In the first month of the Stink it had become apparent that government was powerless to act. Each bureaucratic subdivision in turn declared that the river was not in their jurisdiction. It seemed clear that the Metropolitan Board of Works should be responsible for the problem, but it was also clear that the board lacked authority to deal with the Thames.

The Board of Works is an excellent example of the institution-generating capacity of environmental crises. Prior to the Stink, jurisdictional areas were determined wholly by the physical disposition of sewers and drains. Authority over the river was, however, separate from any city district government. The board was only given full control over metropolitan drainage in 1858, under the acute, formidable, and direct stimulus of the Stink.

In 1865, an interceptor system was completed which diverted central London sewage to the surrounding countryside. The relationship between pollution and disease was still a matter of heated controversy, however, and chemical and engineering solutions to water problems were still believed to be the only effective courses of action. The problem was simply exported to others less fortunate outside London's jurisdiction. Recurrent waterborne disease problems were not addressed until later, and then only after enormous public outcry.

The Great Stink illuminates a number of conclusions which are applicable to the present situation in America. First, environmental crises involving water invite technical and managerial responses at each point in the system. Appropriate interest groups attack the problem, but their piecemeal approach does little to eliminate the root causes of the problem. The response is therapeutic rather than prophylactic.

Second, the managerial response, whether local or national, depends on perception of an acute crisis state for its initial stimulus. Solutions, even if available, are usually not applied without powerful stimulus.

Third, the crisis must be of sufficient magnitude to be perceived as a threat to the security of those entrusted with the power to effect change. It must, in effect, be so graphic that it catches the public fancy, so that to ignore it would be an act of political suicide.

Fourth, scientific and technological responses to water crises vary with disciplinary perspectives. Given a choice, that scientific analysis which is most harmonious with the immediate aims and values of the extant power structure will guide water resource management decisions.

Our current water crisis, if examined closely, meets these four criteria with unsettling accuracy. It remains to be seen if we, like Victorian London, will meet our current dilemma with piecemeal, politically expedient, and ineffective technological fixes, or if the rigors of the present situation are sufficiently recognized as essential and generate mandatory correction by real change on the parts of citizens and their governing institutions.

The Historical Development of Water Problems in America

The history of man in North America contains many elements of environmental crisis and response common to cultures previously discussed. Our path is still in the making, however, and we have only recently reached the critical crossroads in our societal development. Introspection is sometimes difficult. Nevertheless, we must realize that the history of America is best viewed as a story of continual expansion into and subsequent exploitation of virgin territories by immigrant populations and the ramifications of this ethic when unexploited territories ceased to exist.

We know that European man found in North America a rich and varied land with a marvelously complex biota. In direct contrast to the chronic shortages of arable land, water, and other resources of his native continent, he saw a chance to renew the expansionist ethic which had consumed Europe during the late Middle Ages. The sheer vastness of unexploited land must have been a powerful intoxicant to people so long accustomed to chronic resource limitations. We know that in just a few centuries, European man has reduced the complexity and variety of the American landscape and that the expansionist ethic has run out of fodder for further expansion.

The first of the Europeans found in America a wilderness, a place that frightened the timid and challenged the adventurous. The new settlers saw the wilderness as a place to tame and saw it as their given right and duty to exploit nature. For most of the history of the United States, the wilderness has been with us. It was always beyond the settlements, or over the horizon, and thus a factor in life and a subconscious influence upon the outlook of man. As we shall see, even as little as ten years ago, it was generally believed, that, save for the possible exception of oil, real resource limitation, particularly in terms of water, was something America was unlikely to see until well into the twenty-first century.

Today, we must face the fact that the old wilderness and its unlimited resource base are gone forever. We must understand the societal forces which brought us to our present water resource situation. If it happens that with knowledge will come wisdom, then, as Bronowski has said, our environment need not become "a trap in time as well as space" for our society.[12]

Early Attitudes and Actions

The individualistic tradition so treasured in the United States was dominant in pioneer America. Individual competition for power, personal wealth, or simply a place in the sun has been responsible for a great deal of environmental degradation, but has also resulted in an unprecedented standard of living. Accompanying this tradition, there has always been an American social consciousness, which has worked to prevent, alleviate, or repair environmental damage. The history of pioneer America, and indeed, of our own time, is a record of the struggle between these two views. Throughout most of our history, the frontier ethic of individual freedom has prevailed.

The idea of environmental constraints on American society is not one usually associated with America's past. The pervasive view is one of rapid and steady expansion, of growth based on almost unlimited natural wealth, and on heavy reliance on water resources to exploit this wealth. Benjamin Franklin was typical of early observers when he noted that Americans could for countless generations escape the constant struggle which characterized European life. He earnestly believed that Americans were blessed with a continent sufficiently rich in resources for this society to be largely immune from population pressures. Instead of causing struggle and restrictions, the American environment could not act as a limiting factor. It was hard at the time to deny his logic.

A typical expression of optimism was written by a visitor to the Mississippi Valley who wrote:

> Our inheritance is beyond our comprehension, our climate superior, our country bounded by oceans and traversed by noble rivers and lakes. . . . Where can we find our country's equal in geographical and natural advantages, in material progress, or in general prosperity? As a united and free people, the United States presents to the nations of the world a spectacle that we must excite the grandest wonder and admiration.[13]

Indeed. And if we were impressed, think of the impact on the Europeans still struggling with overcrowding and mean lives on their continent. The possibilities afforded by the wealth of our natural environment were almost incomprehensible within the context of the European experience, at least during the previous several hundred years. The intoxicating promise of a better life produced an enormous tide of immigrants to this country.

What part did America's water resources play in the expansion and colonization of America? First, settlement patterns always dictated that sites be chosen which were near navigational water bodies. The eastern coast of America was colonized initially at sites which afforded natural harbors where large rivers emptied into the ocean. When settlements pushed westward, they were generally located near fortifications, which themselves were nearly always at the confluence of major river systems or, later, at strategic points on the Great Lakes. Since water supplies for drinking and agriculture were nearly always abundant, water policy in pioneer America was largely concerned with transportation. Roads were scarce, and even after the development of rail transportation, water transport was still an economic necessity. Channel improvement on the Mississippi and Ohio and other major rivers, along with vast canal building projects, especially in Ohio and New York, absorbed much of the attention from state and federal governments as well as private ventures. The sole purpose, then, of any environmental action concerning water was to facilitate economic development of underdeveloped regions.[14] The development of water transportation routes in the agricultural West was one of the most prominent features of Henry Clay's "American System" which combined an emphasis on western development with tariff protection for the growing but still fledgling industries of the Northeast.

During nearly the whole of the nineteenth century, public policy and individual attitude were characterized by a relative abundance of resources, particularly water. The chief problems were the adequacy of manpower and the capital to exploit the rich and varied resource base. However, by as early as the close of the nineteenth century, it was becoming abundantly clear that America's promise of unlimited resources was faltering.

After several decades of unrestricted commercial hunting, large game animals had become virtually extinct east of the Mississippi. Herds of buffalo on the plains were near extinction. The demise of the passenger pigeon was just around the corner.

On the coast, fisherman witnessed drastic decreases in fish harvest from nearshore waters. By 1870, commercial fishermen were already forced to deeper waters offshore to catch reasonable quantities of fish.

At the same time, deforestation was taking its toll on both the timber industry and agriculture. A paper presented to the American Association for the Advancement of Science in 1873 suggested that unless existing timber harvesting practices were halted immediately, the nation's forests would be destroyed within the century. Total, complete deforestation of entire states, such as Michigan, was accomplished within a few decades.

From the West, Americans received reports that the undeveloped territories were not the promised lands once believed. John Wesley Powell issued an official government report which indicated that, while the western territories had great potential, capital requirements would virtually exclude small entrepreneurs from its development. Chief among these difficulties was the paucity of surface water in these regions, which made both transportation and agriculture difficult. By the turn of the century, the Bureau of the Census officially announced that the unsettled frontier on the continent no longer existed. This conclusion should have impressed on Americans, more than shortages of any single resource, that the limits of growth were already being reached. Such a realization, however, was only dimly perceived.

One of the forces which further accelerated resource problems, particularly in the industrial cities of the East and the Great Lakes region, was the development of the American industrial revolution during the last half of the nineteenth century. As technological developments permitted the energy- and resource-intensive mechanization of industry, urban areas experienced increased demands on their abilities to provide basic services such as water to their inhabitants. Spurred by the promise of jobs, immigration to large industrial cities became a tidal wave. Cities such as Chicago, Detroit, and Cleveland experienced phenomenal growth. Despite the fact that many of these urban areas were located near large bodies of fresh water, especially in the Great Lakes region, demand for water far outstripped the supply capacity of municipal systems. Nascent industries required large amounts of water for production of goods and the electrification of industry produced further environmental problems. Rather rapidly, urban areas developed sewage and water supply problems similar to those found in Victorian London. Civic responses to these new problems were also similar to the

London experience. Water closets were added to houses and raw sewage ended up in rivers and in adjacent lakes. By the turn of the century, Lake Erie, Lake Ontario, and the southern basin of Lake Michigan were noticeably polluted. By 1890, the Atlantic salmon had already become extinct in Lake Ontario.

The late nineteenth century saw the development of four major ideas concerning society and the environment, each with a wide following. These major modes of thought may be characterized as conservation, preservation, ecology, and laissez-faire. Because of the varying goals of proponents of these concepts, widespread reform to solve environmental problems, particularly those involving water, was generally impossible.

Scientific and technical advances had proceeded to the point where policy makers were becoming aware of the web of interaction among resources, for example among the land and water resources of the Mississippi Valley. These concerns were still motivated by economic considerations. By the turn of the century, the concept of multipurpose resource development had been formulated for water and related land resources. Flood control, navigation, watershed protection, irrigation, and even electric power generation were viewed as purposes whose development should be sought on an integrated basis.

Around the turn of the century, conservation received the greatest publicity. Its spokesmen were the most vocal and political. Conservationists promised to meet environmental crises with minimal modification of existing American society. Importantly, conservationists believed that application of scientific and technical knowledge could forestall promised resource shortfalls and that the status quo could thus be maintained. As practical programs developed, beginning with the appearance of the United States Fish Commission in 1871 and the Division of Forestry in 1881, Congress passed a number of laws to protect natural resources from exploitation.

By 1900, however, conservationists confronted a dilemma. Their piecemeal approach to conservation practices yielded only limited results. While they could respond to problems as they arose, the number and complexity of increasingly interrelated environmental problems mounted. In the first decade of the twentieth century, their ideas were encouraged by the leadership of President Theodore Roosevelt, and attempts at reform were implemented. In 1908, the president called together a conference of governors to secure congressional support for a new environmental initiative. Roosevelt warned the governors that without quick measures, the nation's natural wealth was "in danger of exhaustion."[15]

Despite the acquisition of lands destined to become national parks and reserves, and the passage of the Land Reclamation Program, fragmentation among the ranks kept the conservationists from being very successful. Everyone realized that a unified general policy for resource management was sorely needed, but no one could agree as to who should do the managing and whose purpose should be served by it. In short, there was no agreement as to who constituted society or what defined social interest.

In proposing a greater role for government in ordering societal relationships to the environment, conservationists, led among others by G. Pinchot and W. J. McGee, were particularly vehement in their attack on individualism and laissez-faire. McGee especially condemned these viewpoints as the two major producers of waste throughout the history of the nation, concluding:

> In all the world's history no other such saturnalia of squandering the sources of permanent prosperity was ever witnessed! In the material aspect, our individual liberty became collective license; the balance between impulse and responsibility was lost, the future of the people and the Nation was forgotten, and the very name of prosperity was made a by-word by men in high places; and worst of all the very profligacies came to be venerated as law and even crystalized foolishly in devisions or more questionably in enactments—and for long they were not to stand in the way of the growing avalanche of extravagance.[16]

"The greatest good for the greatest number for the longest time," a battle cry of early-twentieth-century conservationists, was clearly at odds with such individualism. Of course, this viewpoint flew in the face of the thinking which had built the nation and was staunchly denounced by champions of free enterprise and capitalism. Many government leaders felt that the best solution, especially in the still underdeveloped West, was for the government to develop water resources, provide laws for their effective utilization, and then allow free enterprise unrestricted access to these resources.

This schism deepened when William Howard Taft became president. Taft proved reluctant to push forward the power of the nation at the expense of individuals or states, making a general natural resource policy untenable.

Other individuals at this time felt that natural areas possessed a spiritual quality necessary for the survival of mankind, and argued for wilderness preservation, the preservation of the undeveloped. This idea, of course, was not new, having been espoused by Thoreau, Catlin, and others. By the late nineteenth century, men like Charles Eliot, the president of Harvard University and the chairman of the National Conservation Congress, and John Muir championed the preservationist movement. To them, the city and industrial society created evils too great for the human body to endure, curable only through resort to unspoiled nature. Their views were frequently at odds with the body of conservationists. The split in the conservationist ranks between preservationists and technological-scientific conservationists weakened their total effects against the status quo power structure and rendered the group as a whole largely ineffective. While preservationists were and still are instrumental in fostering legislation aimed at saving natural areas, they did little in the early twentieth century to advance national resource policy.

The third approach to the resource crises of the late nineteenth century embraced elements of both conservationism and preservationism, but had unique elements which would make its adherents uncooperative with those of the other two philosophies. This approach may be called ecological. Ecologists viewed man as an integral part of nature and believed that the demands of nature as well as the demands of man must play equal roles in policy decisions. The earliest proponent of this view in the United States was George P. Marsh, a diplomat who had served in Europe and had witnessed firsthand the devastation that resulted from ignoring the demands of nature. Marsh viewed the European experience as proof of the validity of his views and cautioned Americans not to fall into the same trap. He and others suggested that man really had no right to do with nature as he pleased. This approach was very radical for the times and his band of followers, although comprised of influential academicians, was small. Their small size as a group forced them to move slowly and their perception of themselves as adversaries to the rest of the community proved highly unpopular.

Ecologists, in short, felt they had the truth and the rest of society be damned.

If ecologists felt they had a patent on truth, to outsiders this particular approach bordered on heresy. It attacked not only traditional societal and economic views, but also religious tenets and basic views about life itself. Ecologists attacked man's conceit, his belief in himself as the lord of his environment, and man's relationship to the plants and animals around him which he had too readily destroyed for his own convenience.

The ecological view, as a whole, proved too radical for general acceptance. The ecologists of the time lacked hard data to back up their claims and too often retreated to evangelism rather than hard reasoning to demonstrate the wisdom of their perspectives.

Despite the best efforts of conservationists, preservationists, and early ecologists, no national resource policy emerged. The dominant political policy was still one of laissez-faire—an attitude of "let the situation develop and see what happens." Accompanying this view was an underlying optimism that nature or God would always work things out. Intervention, especially by government, was seen as ineffective and counterproductive. While immediate, acute shortages might result, existing institutions, particularly those in the private sector, would meet the crises.

The ideology of the advocates of laissez-faire represented a reassertion of traditional American ideas. The environment existed for man to subdue and develop by private initiative, by the individual whose pursuit of his own interests worked for the interests of the American people.

As America entered the twentieth century, resources were diminishing, both in total supply and in quality. Water in cities became increasingly polluted and great riverways were clogged with debris. Everyone could see that something was happening but no consensus emerged as to what could or should be done. What had emerged was more of a political than scientific or technological dilemma in which a variety of views, each purporting to represent the best interests of the United States, fought for support. Perhaps by default, laissez-faire won out. During both Roosevelt's and Taft's administrations, proposals put before Congress to address real resource problems were rebuffed. Private interests, forming powerful special interest groups, succeeded in ousting government officials who transgressed against states' rights.

No broad reform plan emerged, no comprehensive solution to any problems evolved. Instead, the nation met crises as it and other cultures had done in the past, piecemeal and responsively. This direction placed the power of adjustment directly into the hands of those tied to specific shortages. Thus, power companies built dams which changed the water flow and cycling processes of whole watersheds, steel companies sought new sources of iron ore and shipped them over waterways as they pleased, and so on. Public policy which was formulated during the early years of the twentieth century was directed at these goals. The Federal Power Act (1920), for instance, established federal licensing for private development of water-power sites.

In the short run, these policies of "no policy at all" proved effective. Private industry and enterprise were, for profit motives, interested in efficient resource utilization, and managed to develop waterways projects which seemed at the time to directly address a number of water resource problems. But these good effects were only short-term.

The discovery and rapid exploitation of new resources again spurred American growth, and, as before, the expanding American populace and its demands quickly absorbed any surpluses. Thus, society was still tied to the same pattern of resource management which had led to crisis in the first place. During the 1920s, private enterprise gained enormous control over the American resource base. Importantly, the very idea which laissez-faire had sought to eliminate was brought to fruition; individuals had lost economic and political control. The fate of natural resources essential to life was largely in the control of private interests.

America after the Great Depression

As the Depression of the 1930s forced enormous changes in public economic policy, so too did it result in a major period of creative thinking in the resource field. The laissez-faire economic and resource policy had resulted in the worst economic disruption in the nation's history. Individuals were clamoring for government to do something. American cities were showing signs of deterioriation. Several years of drought coupled with poor land use practices fostered the Dust Bowl era in the most important agricultural regions of the country.

Responding again to the symptoms rather than the disease, the Roosevelt administration fostered a broad-based public policy regarding land and water resources. Soil conservation on a broad scale, the Civilian Conservation Corps, the Tennessee Valley Authority, and many other policies were launched with varying success to stem both the tide of environmental degradation and general economic malaise. These programs seemed to be meeting with success when the world was again plunged into war.

World War II profoundly influenced resource planning from the late forties until the present day. Returning servicemen and their progeny of the Baby Boom became the most prolific consumers of resources in American history. Thousands of new towns and suburbs were quickly built to accommodate the burgeoning need for housing. Municipal systems were hard pressed to meet this increased demand for sewage removal and water supply.

Consequently, most postwar housing developments, particularly in suburban and rural areas, were built with septic systems and individual wells rather than being tied in to central sewage and water supply systems. This arrangement put further burdens on groundwater supplies and on the sewage loading to subsurface aquifers and surface water supplies.

To provide land needed for housing, more and more forest areas were cut down and wetlands drained. Erosion and subsequent degradation of existing rivers and lakes and the disruption of normal groundwater recharge processes soon occurred near large housing projects, shopping centers, and the other demand concentrations.

To supply food needed to fuel the population expansions, farmers were increasingly called upon to put marginal land into production. Semiarid land required extensive irrigation, and much of the irrigation water was drawn from already stressed groundwater supplies. Wise land use practices fostered by the Dust Bowl experience were increasingly ignored as farmers put every available acre of land to use in monoculture. Importantly, the "Green Revolution," touted in the 1960s as the scientific breakthrough which would forever rid the world of famine, was predicated on the development of strains of crops which would produce high yields only with increased water, fertilizer, and energy subsidies.

Demographic patterns changed drastically after World War II. Increasingly, people fled the crowded but water-rich cities of the urban Midwest to what they perceived as greater opportunity in chronically water-poor regions of the West and Southwest. Communities were ill prepared for this invasion. This second mass redistribution of population was far greater in magnitude than the population relocation noted during the industrial revolution of the nineteenth century. By the 1950s and 1960s, much of the West and Southwest experienced chronic water shortages. Poorly blessed with surface waters, these areas had to rely almost exclusively on groundwater. As people, industry, and, increasingly, irrigated agriculture crowded into the Sun Belt, water tables were driven lower and lower each year. As water was withdrawn, whole communities slumped as the land settled beneath them. The San Joaquin Valley subsided almost 30 feet from the 1930s to the 1960s. Increasingly, farmers noted that their soil was becoming damagingly saline, the result of salt residues left from evaporating irrigation water.

As population expanded exponentially and moved increasingly into already ecologically sensitive water-poor habitats, technological growth and its concomitant demands on water also increased exponentially. Each person, then, consumed more and more water on a per capita basis, as water-intensive agriculture and industrial techniques added to physiological and residential usage.

During the expansionist postwar era, technology became fixed in its present-day role as a panacea for all mankind's problems. Technological cures were seen as a means of eliminating problems caused by burgeoning demands on declining water resources. The country which conquered others on a worldwide basis could certainly devise alternatives needed to "solve" water resource problems. Actual *shortages* of something as basic as water were quite unthinkable.

As late as the mid-1960s, resource scarcity, particularly water scarcity, was seen as a problem which would not be felt until the twenty-first century, if at all. The landmark Landsburg, Fischman, and Fisher analysis of 1963[17] did not discover any resource scarcity so critical that it threatened to retard the development of the continental economy during the twentieth century. By implication, no habitat is in danger due to crises of scarcity. Fisher further noted in 1966:

> Undoubtedly, demand for water will increase considerably in the years ahead as it has in past decades. Here again improvements in management of water supply, such as treatment and reuse, can make it possible for fairly large increases in demand to be met without severe general problems of shortage. In the eastern part of the United States plentiful rainfall evenly distributed indicates that the chief problem will not be one of supply. . . . In the West the chief problem will probably remain that of assuring sufficient

supplies, but even in quite arid places, some shift in use away from irrigation toward municipal and industrial uses would make possible a continued population increase and industrial development.[18]

During the 1960s we, like our predecessors during the nineteenth century, were confident that no problem was unsolvable given American effort and ingenuity. Each analysis of resource bases compiled during these expansionist years projected continuous increases in population, technological growth, and improved standard of living far into the twenty-first century.

Environmental degradation itself was, until the late 1960s, also not thought to pose much of a problem. Despite the fact that many lakes and most rivers were already grossly polluted by the 1960s, it was generally believed that in only a "limited number of resources there may be instances of irreversible destruction, but in most instances expanding technology . . . could increase the supply and, what is more important, achieve better distribution, which would overcome the present appearances of scarcity."[19]

As noted earlier, human populations do not reach full resource utilization capacity until after adolescence. When the children of the late 1940s and early 1950s reached maturity, the fallacies of these predictions became apparent. We began to see that environmental degradation of existing water supplies coupled with exponentially increasing demand on water reserves were beginning to cause real, highly visible problems. Beaches on the Great Lakes were closed to swimming because of bacterial contamination. The Cuyahoga River in Cleveland caught fire. The Southwest was reeling from the effects of one water crisis after another. Wells all over the United States, especially in the Southwest, plains, and coastal areas, began drying and new, deeper wells had to be drilled. Saline water was intruding from the sea into depleted groundwater aquifers in certain coastal regions.

By the late 1970s, grandiose projects were being seriously proposed to redistribute water from areas of surplus to arid regions. Since California had long since "annexed" the Colorado River basin, it turned attention to northern California and even as far as Canada, and proposed massive pipeline projects to divert water to agriculture, industry, and people. With the exception of a few ecologists,[20] few accepted the obvious fact that *technological expansion was one of the prime causes of water shortfalls, rather than the potential cure.* The energy shortages and their effects on northern industrial cities further intensified the flight of people to the Sun Belt. Nearly every geographical area in the plains, Far West, Southeast, and Southwest was now withdrawing water from surface and groundwater supplies faster than it was being replaced.

As America enters the 1980s, more and more instances of acute contamination of surface and groundwater by toxic wastes, acid rain, and saline intrusion emerge. Legislation in the 1970s had focused on water pollution, specifically in areas of eutrophication (see chap. 4). But water pollution and eutrophication are only facets of a much larger problem. The large-scale water problems now facing the United States, as in other cultures, have simply not been addressed. Cultural forces in the United States have produced environmental problems and addressed these problems in the most politically expedient and unobtrusive way. Consequently, major water-related problems have not been solved. We as a nation have let things run their course and have concentrated our efforts on intermediate and politically attractive facets of complex problems.

The time has come when the frontier ethic must forever disappear from our social and political mores. We can no longer call on technology to come up with more water to fuel ever-expanding population, technological, and agricultural demands. We have generally reached, and in regions exceeded, the break-even point in our water economy. The lessons of history are clear. A society cannot long exceed its environmental carrying capacity, particularly in terms of an absolutely essential resource like water. Inevitably, demand must decrease, either through wise and efficient utilization or through catastrophe. As a country, we are living on borrowed time, as we consume in months water which will take years to replenish even under ideal conditions, and continually increase the degradation of those supplies that do exist. America is drying and most realistic appraisals suggest that things will get a good deal dryer in the future. For the first time in our history, we must make the right choices; our standard of living and role as a world leader hinge on these decisions.

Alarmist and inflammatory rhetoric accomplishes little. Experience in our own culture shows that this approach is counterproductive. In the case of our shrinking water resource base, there can be no argument that a rational approach to reducing water demand is both politically and economically expedient *and* in the best interests of the American individual. Our choice is simple. Either we make some fundamental changes in the way in which we view water as an integrated component of our society or we will relinquish control over a vital part of our individual freedom and societal future.

NOTES

1. J. R. Vallentyne, "Freshwater Supplies and Pollution: Effects of the Demophoric Explosion on Water and Man," in *The Environmental Future*, ed. N. Polunin (London: Macmillan and Co., 1972), pp. 181–211.

2. T. R. Malthus, "Essay on the Principle of Population as It Affects the Future of Society." (1798), reprinted as *Population: The First Essay* (Ann Arbor: University of Michigan Press, 1959). Numerous writers have recognized the relationships of human population to resource availability. Malthus's classical predictions have been echoed by many contemporary authors. A good overview of population-resource interactions can be obtained in any general ecology textbook. Historical implications for human population dynamics can be found in *Historical Ecology*, an excellent short book on environment and social change, edited by L. J. Bilsky (Port Washington, N.Y.: Kennikat Press, 1980).

3. R. A. Bryson and T. J. Murray, *Climates of Hunger* (Madison: University of Wisconsin Press, 1977), pp. 19–20.

4. Ibid., pp. 19–44.

5. L. J. Bilsky, "Ecological Crisis and Response in Ancient China," in *Historical Ecology*, ed. Bilsky, pp. 60–70.

6. Ibid., p. 67.

7. C. R. Bowlus, "Ecological Crisis in Fourteenth Century Europe," in *Historical Ecology*, ed. Bilsky, pp. 86–99.

8. P. Ziegler, *The Black Death* (London: Penguin Books, 1970).

9. Bryson and Murray, *Climates of Hunger*.

10. T. F. Glick, "Science, Technology, and the Urban Environment: The Great Stink of 1858," in *Historical Ecology,* ed. Bilsky, p. 123.

11. Ibid., pp. 122–39.

12. J. Bronowski, *The Ascent of Man,* (Boston: Little, Brown and Co., 1973). Biological evolution works to produce a species which is highly adapted to a specific environment. If the environment changes, specific adaptations to that environment cease to be beneficial. Unlike many animals, man is a generalist, not particularly adapted to any single environment. If the physical environment changes, it becomes a trap in space as well as time for the specialist. Man's cultural evolution permits him to escape these problems—to escape the consequences of biological evolution.

13. C. H. Moneyhan, "Environmental Crisis and American Politics, 1860–1920," in *Historical Ecology*, ed. Bilsky, p. 141; see also M. V. Melosi, ed.,

Pollution and Reform in American Cities, 1870–1930 (Austin: University of Texas Press, 1980).

14. J. L. Fisher, "Natural Resources and Economic Development: The Web of Events, Policies, and Policy Objectives," in *Future Environments of North America,* ed. F. Fraser Darling and J. P. Milton (New York: Natural History Press, 1966), pp. 262–88.

15. Fisher, "Natural Resources." The Governors Conference of 1908 was a landmark event, but was, unfortunately, ahead of its time.

16. Moneyhan, "Environmental Crisis," p. 147.

17. H. H. Landsburg, L. L. Fischman, and J. L. Fisher, *Resources in America's Future* (Baltimore: Johns Hopkins Press, 1963), p. 1017; see also R. L. Meier, "Technology, Resources, and Urbanism—The Long View," in *Future Environments of North America,* ed. Darling and Milton, pp. 277–88.

18. Fisher, "Natural Resources," p. 275. Fisher's position on resource limitation or scarcity was echoed by many economists and futurists of the 1960s. Fisher further states that "the age-old concern for resource shortages seems to have boiled away to a scientific-technological-economic-management problem." In hindsight, we can see how different things looked as little as fifteen years ago, before the rise of OPEC and other factors discussed in this book. An excellent review of the effects literary naturalists have had on environmental policy in the United States may be found in P. Brooks, *Speaking for Nature* (New York: Houghton Mifflin Co., 1980).

19. K. E. Boulding, "Economics and Ecology," in *Future Environments of North America,* ed. Darling and Milton, p. 243. Boulding's views, shared by many economists of the period, were reminiscent of J. K. Galbraith in *The Affluent Society* (New York: Houghton Mifflin Co., 1958). Again, while these views were by no means universal, real resource shortfalls, unaddressable by technological means, were seen as a problem only of the far-distant future.

20. Vallentyne, "Freshwater Supplies."

6 Our Present Situation

*It is better never to begin a good work
than, having begun it, to stop.*

Bede

The demand for water by our growing society is already outstripping
the resupply of water to usable sources in many parts of the country.
Exploding demophoric growth contributes to excessive demand and increases the degradation of extant water supplies and the terrestrial
environment so necessary to water recharge. What future routes should
American society take to ameliorate these effects of a water-limited
way of life? What are our options? How can we learn from the water
problem of other cultures and from the mistakes of our recent past?

Our responses to these fundamental questions will in large measure
determine the quality of life and state of individual freedom in American
society well into the next century. Two divergent courses are still possible. We can continue to treat water as we always have, as a resource
without limit, addressing acute, highly visible manifestations of water
resource problems with short-sighted technological fixes, thereby creating new and more serious problems in the future. Alternately, we can
continue to avoid the fact that real water limitation is upon us, confident
that new sources will always become available to slake our thirst for
water.

We have seen that these approaches only postpone the day of
reckoning. Inevitably, a limiting resource by definition becomes insufficient to support the existing society. At that point, nature inexorably
balances the supply and demand equation. For our society, as others
before us, this could only mean inevitable and chaotic cultural decline.
No technology, however powerful, can produce supplies of a resource
which have ceased to exist. To follow our current uncontrolled path is
to invite an ominous and uncertain future, totally incompatible with
our tradition of individual freedom and economic and social opportunity.

This path need not be followed. We, like Dickens's Scrooge, can see our future and act to change it. Our ability as a species to perceive the future and act to change its course has been central to our cultural evolution. This ability can serve us well in dealing with the current and future freshwater crises in America. The outlook need not be grim.

As individuals and as a society, we must finally and irrevocably turn away from a water-intensive economy. The notion that resources like water can be exploited infinitely is a childish one, a viewpoint which has no place in a mature society. We have begun the transition to societal adulthood with regard to our energy policy; we must foster this same spirit in our policy toward water. To do less will constrain our societal options in the future, putting our freedoms and quality of life in jeopardy as well as those of the millions around the world dependent on the United States for sustenance. Our problems are clear, addressable, solvable, and infinitely preferable to projected conditions in future America if we defer action now.

Our Present Course: Where Will It Lead?

What specifically will happen to the quality of life in the United States if our present water resource strategy remains unaltered? To answer this question, we must consider several factors which enter into the water resource balance equation. These factors include projected population increases, changes in both the demographic distribution of population and the relative rate of continued demophoric growth, and the intangible factor of potential climatic change.

Many projections of future water demand have appeared in the last several years. All are predicated on the projection of future water demand based on certain baseline data. For this reason, many such predictions quickly become obsolete, as unforeseen complications arise which render untenable the underlying assumptions of the model.

In 1973, the National Water Commission presented to the United States Congress a comprehensive and detailed analysis of a number of "alternate water futures" covering the period from the 1970s to 2020.[1] These projections were based on currently available data and reflected presumed ranges in a number of variables which would affect the water supply and demand equation. Their report concluded that, given adequate planning and preparation, American agricultural, industrial, and residential water needs could easily be met well into the early years of the twenty-first century. In hindsight, we can see how the unforeseen Arab oil embargo and subsequent precipitous increases in energy costs and the marked shifts in population demographics in the 1970s effectively short-circuited such optimistic appraisals. By the late 1970s, it was clear that our national water policies had to be fundamentally altered, leading in part to the Clean Water Act of 1977 and the Carter administration's 1978 proposals for sweeping changes in water policy initiatives.

Such radical changes in the perception of our national water position, even within a brief span of time, exemplify the types of problems encountered by resource planners dealing with water. It would seem prudent to view the present water situation in the United States and its ramifications for the future within the broadest possible range of conditions. Let us examine some of the specifics of American water futures, beginning first by projecting a future based on inaction and allowing present trends to run their course.

Although American population is increasing, the rate of growth has slowed in recent years. It is unlikely that the United States population will approach the figure of 330 million predicted by the turn of the century in several studies of the 1960s. Nonetheless, it is clear that our population will continue to expand, albeit at a slower rate of increase, so that approximately 275 million people will inhabit the continental United States by the year 2050.[2] The actual increment of population increase may be higher if women who postponed having children in the 1970s decide to begin families in the 1980s. Keeping in mind that these new citizens will not reach full resource utilization capacity until the late 1990s and into the first years of the twenty-first century, we can conclude that demand for water based solely on physiological need would undoubtedly escalate in the coming years.

The physiological need for water constitutes only a small proportion of actual individual water usage. From our discussion of demophoric growth, we know that each new individual would require proportionately greater amounts of water in agriculture, for residential needs, and to fuel the technological machine which generates necessary products. As more marginal lands are put into food production and increasing quantities of water are used for power generation and energy production, per capita water usage must increase markedly. Thus, each succeeding increment of population increase would produce proportionately greater demands on water resources, as supplies become more difficult to exploit.

The total population has a direct bearing, then, on potential water utilization capacity. We can only conclude that if current per capita consumption practices continue, the drain on water resources, already exploited beyond the break-even point in some parts of the country, will increase still further.

Yet the total population is only one factor in projected water resource utilization. We know that the demographic distribution of population, agricultural, and industrial centers in relation to water distribution is even more important than total population size.

Population migrations have been a part of the history of the United States. The westward migration continues from the earliest days of our history. The southward demographic migration began in earnest about 1910 and accelerated since 1940, with a simultaneous migration from rural areas to cities, from villages to metropolitan areas, and within metropolitan areas, movement from city centers to residential suburban areas.

Between 1970 and 1974, unprecedented southward migration occurred. Ten of the thirteen largest metropolitan areas, all northern and eastern cities except Los Angeles, experienced net population migration out of the urban areas.[3] The three largest cities experiencing major net positive population growth were all located in the South, all in areas of exisiting water limitations. This migration trend that began in earnest in the 1970s will be unquestionably short-lived—initiated by energy constraints, terminated by freshwater constraints. As our society matures into a highly efficient energy user and recycler of resources, a shift toward clustered, attached, and high-rise housing and industrial groupings may develop, surrounded by community-owned open lands for agriculture, recreation, and natural reserves.[4] Such planned communities are already being developed (see chap. 8).

We have repeatedly emphasized the concept of demophoric growth as it relates to water consumption and degradation. In addition to added population pressure and demographic distributional changes, we would project that the current unchecked growth of the technological complex would only intensify acute and chronic water resource problems in the years ahead. Currently, we still view technology as a potential savior in water crises. As in energy shortfalls, water problems are themselves spawned in large measure by the uncontrolled, exploitive demophoric growth of our society. If the present trend is not ameliorated, such growth would only be checked by catastrophic freshwater resource limitation. Enormous expenses would be incurred both in the acquisition of water from increasingly distant and depleted sources and in the treatment of water degraded by human activities. The U.S. Environmental Protection Agency's 1978 needs survey estimated that $36 billion would be required to construct necessary secondary treatment and advanced wastewater treatment facilities in order to update facilities to present standards.[5] The same study fixed the cost of controlling pollution from combined sewer overflows and storm runoff from existing urban areas at $26 billion and $62 billion, respectively. If water usage and subsequent degradation are allowed to escalate, these costs will consume increasingly large portions of our gross national product, further reducing economic productivity. With the current nationwide trend toward reduced taxes, we cannot expect to continually increase the demands on municipal water supply and treatment facilities without seriously affecting water quality. Simply stated, the responsibility for purified water use and return to the environment must be accepted; its costs now are much less than those in the future once contaminants are dispersed.

More toxic waste dumps are discovered each year. Further, the production of new organic compounds for use in agriculture and industry continues to intensify. The exploitation of energy reserves in hitherto underdeveloped regions like the American West is scheduled to boom in coming years. Each of these factors dictate that unless our current policies are changed, the degradation of land and water will reach epidemic and perhaps uncontrollable proportions in the near future. We have seen that once contaminants are dispersed in the environment, they become exceedingly difficult to remove and then only at great expense to consumers of water. Should the present trend continue, it may be difficult to find directly utilizable fresh water in many large areas of the United States by the end of the century.

It was not until 1976 and the passage of the Resource Conservation and Recovery Act (PL 94–580) that the hazardous waste challenge was given top priority in the federal regulatory program. We have begun to implement this challenge, both on an individual and governmental level, but the magnitude of environmental degradation problems has rendered full compliance with the letter and intent of recent laws ineffectual. Within the present power structure, water problems such as acid rain, toxic waste, and groundwater contamination which extend across state and national boundaries are difficult to deal with. However, to defer intensifying efforts to isolate contamination *at the source* would effectively eliminate any hope of stemming the avalanche of water degradation problems.

Long-distance transport of water to parched, high-demand areas is a dubious strategy of considerable cost and limited benefits. Nonetheless, redistribution schemes within certain geographical areas appear necessary to supply needed water for built-in and projected increases in demand foreseen into the next century.[6] Careful studies in many southern and western regions indicate that more efficient water utilization and recycling techniques may be insufficient to balance supply and demand forecasts for the next several decades. These studies collectively assert that efficient, comprehensive water resource strategies require cooperation between individuals, governmental units, and the industrial-agricultural complex. Tacit in this cooperative action is the realization by all of these entities of the futility of our present water resource strategy, the inevitable and considerable costs of necessary changes, and most importantly, the short- and long-term economic and social benefits accruing from these changes.

In projecting our future water economy, we must remember that climatic change would fundamentally alter the actual amount of water available to our society, a factor greatly underappreciated by citizens and government alike. The potential for climatically induced water shortfalls is real and must be recognized. Since we cannot predict the direction of future climatic change, we cannot continue extant policies based on the relatively high rainfall pattern of the last several decades. From climatological and meteorological data it is clear that the actual supplies of fresh water available to us in coming years may be drastically curtailed by processes beyond our control.

Current Individual and Governmental Attitudes about Water Problems

Before a society can write or enforce environmental laws and policy, it must have a clearly defined environmental ethic. A decade or so after Earth Day, what attitudes do Americans have about environmental crises in general and water problems specifically? On the one hand, our individual attitudes bode well for the future.[7] We are cognizant of the interrelated nature of environmental problems, of the political, social, and scientific components. We are largely convinced that energy conservation and development of alternative energy sources are important priority items.

However, a number of disturbing trends are still evident. We as a society still retain faith in the technological approach to solving environmental problems and in the adequacy of present laws and conventions governing the use of natural resources. We are apt to believe that economic growth must, by definition, supplant concern for resource exploitation; that what is good for business is good for us. There is a feeling that economic growth and wise use of resources, particularly water, are somehow incongruous. Importantly, we feel that energy shortfalls dwarf any other foreseeable resource limitations and that the solution of energy problems, by whatever means necessary, represents our only pressing national resource problem. While we recognize a sense of individual responsibility for environmental problems, individuals still do not clearly see the critical role man plays is the dynamics of water in the hydrosphere. A consciousness of water as a precious and fundamentally important limiting resource has been slow to develop. The inadequacy of piecemeal technological solutions to water problems is still not generally recognized.

These individual attitudes are reflected in similar perspectives in government. We have been so preoccupied with the energy crisis that water limitation has more or less crept up on us. Government policy is still directed largely at the construction of large water management projects—dams, river channelization projects, and the like. The propensity of government agencies to spend money on huge technological water projects has brought numerous benefits to the United States. We must realize, however, that no reservoir impoundment, pipeline project, or water distribution scheme can produce more water—it can only redistribute the water that is there. Furthermore, many sanctioned projects, particularly those dealing with rechannelization of rivers, actually diminish water resupply patterns by increasing system flow-through and erosion rates.

Coping with energy and mineral resources will by necessity evolve to an everyday situation of unprecedented efficiency and recycling. Use of energy per person will decrease by at least 50 percent by the middle of the twenty-first century simply by efficient use of energy sources in residential, industrial, and agricultural functions.[8] It will also be necessary for mineral resources to be recycled to an extent difficult to comprehend under present wasteful usage patterns, where existing natural resources are used only to make up for minor losses in manufacturing and use processes.[9] The foremost attitude that must be changed, both individually and by governmental leadership, is that contemporary growth rates are neither necessary nor desirable to maintain a high standard of living. Indeed, the constant growth stance is not only impossible in the long term, but will only work against a balanced use of existing resources in an efficient, integrated society. The more strongly the impossible growth syndrome is pushed, the more rapid and severe will be the certain effects of these limitations of our real world.

The same attitudes of efficient use and intensive recycling of fresh water must evolve. The economics of doing otherwise will be as severe as the energy limitations now coming to the forefront. Indeed, energy and mineral resource limitations cannot be separated from freshwater limitations. Fresh water is the ultimate of our finite resources. Its use must be an integrated component of all resource utilization.

NOTES

1. W. Viessman, Jr. and C. DeMoncada, *State and National Water Use Trends to the Year 2000*, a report prepared by the Congressional Research Service for the U.S. Senate, Serial No. 96–12 (Washington, D.C.: U.S. Government Printing Office, 1980).

2. Bureau of the Census, Department of Commerce, *Statistical Abstract of the United States*, U.S. Census, Series II-X, Projection 1980–2050 (Washington, D.C.: Government Printing Office, 1977).

3. J. S. Stewart et al., "A Low Energy Scenario for the United States: 1975–2050," in *Perspectives on Energy: Issues, Ideas, and Environmental Dilemmas*, ed. L. C. Ruedisili and M. W. Firebaugh (New York: Oxford University Press, 1978), pp. 553–80.

4. Ibid.; see also G. T. Seaborg, "The Recycle Society of Tomorrow," *The Futurist* 8 (1974):108–15.

5. U.S. Environmental Protection Agency, *1978 Needs Survey—Cost Estimates for Construction of Publicly Owned Wastewater Treatment Facilities*, EPA 430/9–79–001 (FRD–1) (Washington, D.C.: U.S. Environmental Protection Agency, 1979); F. W. Ellis and R. L. Wycoff, "Cost-effective Water Quality Planning for Urban Areas," *Journal of Water Pollution Control Federation* 53, no. 3(1981):246–58.

6. Oklahoma Water Resources Board, *Oklahoma Comprehensive Water Plan,* Publication 94, April 1, 1980; D. Sheridan, "The Underwatered West: Overdrawn at the Well," *Environment* 23 (1981):6–33.

7. L. P. Gerlach and B. Radcliffe, "Terrible Questions Provoke Great Responses," *Natural History,* 89, no. 11 (1980):30–34; B. Radcliffe and L. P. Gerlach, "The Ecology Movement After Ten Years," *Natural History* 90 (1981):12–18; R. H. White-Stevens, "The Environmental Ethic," *Fisheries* 1, no. 3 (1976):11–14.

8. Stewart, "Low Energy Scenario"; Seaborg, "Recycle Society."

9. Seaborg, "Recycle Society."

7 Which Way to Go?

No virtue goes with size.

Emerson

Approaches to water problem solving fall into two main categories: (1) *structural/technological*, and (2) *nonstructural*. The former includes high-technology, capital-intensive water projects such as water conveyance systems, reservoir construction, channelization, desalination plants, and similar projects, as well as smaller-scale devices to improve the efficiency of water utilization, such as crop irrigation timers, low-flow shower heads, and domestic wastewater recycling systems. The second type of water problem solving mechanisms is termed nonstructural because they involve changes in attitudes and behavior on the part of water consumers which, without structural modification of water supply systems, effect more conservative utilization of water resources.

As we shall see, a realistic, comprehensive water strategy for future American society must include elements of *both* structural/technological and nonstructural alternatives. Yet, when one examines the immediate past policies and most visible current policies of governmental, industrial, and agricultural agencies, it is evident that the majority of monies and resources at all levels have been concentrated in high-technology, capital-intensive water programs. It is fruitful to examine the details of some of these proposed and realized large-scale structural/technological water crisis solutions.

It would be a gross and unfair oversimplification to denounce all proposed large-scale technologically oriented water supply solutions. But many states and regions are poised on the brink of committing tens of billions of dollars in scarce capital to projects with dubious long-term merit and overstated claims of effectiveness. The massive scale of proposed monetary commitments to such projects has even begun to alarm financial analysts in the business community.[1]

We must agree at the outset that sound regional water planning is an absolute necessity if our water problems are to be effectively addressed. In discussion of water development and conservation strategies, arbitrary political boundaries make little sense. Individual towns or cities simply cannot effectively deal with problems at the watershed or regional water district levels of organization. However, regional water plans which are economically or ecologically irresponsible should be held up to close scrutiny, so that inherent flaws in reasoning can be identified before capital commitments are made. We must realize that when we choose to develop a region chronically poor in water for other pressing reasons, the best we can hope for is a compromise between beneficial and deleterious effects. The electorate, cognizant of the real pros and cons of proposed structural/technological water crisis solutions, should then be the final arbiter on adoption or rejection of such proposals.

Proposed Water Redistribution Schemes

In this section, we discuss some examples of proposed and realized regional water redistribution plans and other proposed water crisis solutions. Our aim is not to denounce certain proposals as being untenable, but rather to demonstrate the trade-offs and potential errors in judgment which inevitably accompany overly simplistic solutions to a complex social, political, and scientific set of problems like the current and future American water crises.

The Central Arizona Project
Reference was made in chapter 3 to the bitter controversy surrounding the partitioning of precious Colorado River water to California and Arizona. The Central Arizona Project is a water redistribution plan aimed at taking full advantage of the recent Supreme Court decision relegating to Arizona a share of water hitherto allocated to California. The plan, scheduled to begin in 1985, is comprised of a $2 billion series of aqueducts and tunnels that resembles a giant plumbing network. If and when this plan is realized, the delicate dynamics of the Colorado River system will be irrevocably altered.[2]

The use of the Colorado was first spelled out in the Colorado River Compact, a document signed by the basin states in 1922. The compact partitioned river water rights into upper and lower basin categories.

This document decreed that the upper basin states of Colorado, New Mexico, Utah, and Wyoming were forever to receive 7.5 million acre-feet of Colorado water per year and the lower basin states of California and Arizona were to receive the same amount. An additional treaty signed in 1944 guaranteed Mexico an additional 1.5 million acre-feet annually, bringing yearly river allotments to 16.5 million acre-feet per year. The problem is that the Colorado rarely carries more than 14.8 million acre-feet of water per year. The resultant overallocation, the source of the Colorado's modern dilemmas, resulted from studies based on an abnormally wet period in the river's history just prior to the signing of the compact. That high-water mark on the Colorado River has not been repeated since.

Up to now, massive water crises in the region have been averted in part because none of the states have insisted on utilizing their full share of Colorado water simultaneously. Nonetheless, in dry years, the compact insures that upper basin states will experience water shortfalls since they are bound by law to allocate the full 7.5 million acre-foot share to the lower basin, regardless of total river flow rates.

However, the Central Arizona Project would provide a situation where demand on the river will finally exceed supply. In carrying Arizona's hitherto incompletely utilized share of Colorado water 300 miles across the desert to Phoenix and Tucson, the overdraft of the Colorado will be complete. It will be impossible for all present commitments to be honored—the river simply does not contain enough water.

The biggest loser in the struggle will be California, the state which currently contributes the least water to Colorado flow but drains the biggest share. When the Central Arizona Project goes on line, California will be faced with a yearly deficit of at least one million acre-feet per year.

There are other losers in the battle for this diminishing resource pie. Five Indian tribes in the dry, red rock country northeast of Los Angeles have militantly campaigned against the Central Arizona Project, claiming that it will deprive them of water guaranteed by a Supreme Court decision. In studies conducted by a lawyer representing the Navajo tribe, whose reservation extends over 25,000 square miles in four basin states, it has been estimated that the Indians could conceivably claim "almost every drop of the Colorado." To avert this scenario, the tribes have proposed a solution to the standoff. Water from the Colorado's newest irrigation district, the Welton-Mohawk near Yuma, Arizona, could be diverted for Indian use. Tribal lawyers argue that no more than fifteen hundred non-Indian farmers would be displaced, while over thirty thousand Indian farmers could be put to work.

Although this solution is abhorrent to Welton-Mohawk farmers who grow a bounty of citrus, wheat, cotton, and alfalfa, one beneficial effect would certainly result. The diversion of irrigation water to the tribal farmlands would counteract the increasing salinity of Colorado River water. Salinity, built up from the evaporation of tons of water in irrigation canals and the agricultural input of minerals, increases as the river flows south. The addition of the Welton-Mohawk irrigation district in the late 1960s represented the salinity increase which broke the river's back. Mexico complained bitterly that its meager share of the Colorado was no longer fit for irrigation. By the time river water crossed the border, its salinity approached 1,500 parts per million, nearly double that of water going to California's rich Imperial valley. In 1973, the U.S. government agreed to a complex formula under which Mexico would receive water no more saline than that delivered to California.

The problem confronting officials was: How could river water salinity be reduced from 1,500 to 800 parts per million? The answer: Build a $350 million desalination plant near Yuma, which represents the ultimate in high technology. The plant would work by reverse osmosis, passing salty Colorado water through a cellulose acetate membrane that traps the salt. A diversion canal built parallel to the river would carry salt residues to the Gulf of California.

We see in the Central Arizona Project the essence of the "technological fix" approach to water problem solving. When a given water resource is insufficient to support demand, almost any large-scale project will be tried to stretch meager supplies still further. At each step of the way, new problems are caused by each "solution." We are just beginning to comprehend the enormity of the complexity of the Colorado River situation. Despite the fact that the physical limits of the river have long been exceeded and its water continues to become more degraded annually, new construction goes on, attempting to coax still more water from nonexistent supplies. Demophoric expansion, fueled by the expectation of heightened water availability, continues to increase. In a panic over the foreseeable future, government officials have seriously contemplated and actually tested cloud seeding experiments designed to induce greater snowfall in the river's headwaters high in the Rocky Mountains. The seeding experiments worked, to the degree that they resulted in many Colorado towns being inundated with 12 feet of snow. Whether even tiny increases in river flow resulted are debatable. What is not debatable is the fact that increasing parts of the Colorado River watershed are being asked to become "national sacrifice areas" in futile attempts to slake the thirst of residents in the lower basin.

The Central Arizona Project and attendant desalination plants, canals, and the like, will not increase the actual regional supply of water, only redistribute meager supplies to temporarily forestall the full magnitude of water shortfall crises. Ultimately, the real and growing shortfall in water supply could produce one of the biggest resource crises this country has yet experienced.

The California State Water Project

That the solution to water crises has in large measure become the domain of engineers and planners is not surprising. But nowhere have these plans become more grandiose than in California.[3] The burgeoning population of southern California coupled with the certainty that a portion of Colorado River water would soon be denied them has fostered a proposed major expansion of California's State Water Project. This project, authorized in 1960, is a classic example of a capital-intensive, energy-intensive structural water crisis solution. It transfers water from northern California to central California, like the federal government's Central Valley Project, which was begun in 1933 and has yet to be completed. To date, about $2.5 billion has been spent in the State Water Project and $3.5 billion on the federal Central Valley Project. Both projects have chiefly benefited agribusiness corporations in the San Joaquin Valley. Many are owned by oil companies (Getty, Standard of California, Shell, and Tenneco) which buy the state water at "bargain basement prices" to irrigate fields of cotton and vegetables. The State Water Project is currently the site's largest single consumer of electricity, using about 4 billion kilowatt hours of electricity per year to pump water around the state.

The California state legislature recently passed legislation (SB 200) that authorizes the building of a major new canal, huge new reservoirs, and related canals. The cost of these facilities, including new power plants they will require, is estimated at $11 billion. The energy cost of pumping water uphill from the system will require an estimated additional 6 billion kilowatt hours of electricity annually by the year 2000.

The centerpiece and most controversial item in the proposed expansion of the State Water Project was the "Peripheral Canal" (voted down in 1982). This 43-mile-long, 400-foot-wide canal would have diverted 70 percent of the flow of the Sacramento River before it reached the San Joaquin–Sacramento River delta east of San Francisco Bay, returned portions of the river's water to the delta at "critical points," and carried the major share around the delta to the extant California Aqueduct for delivery southward. This diversion would have increased by one million acre-feet (nearly 50 percent) the capacity of the flow through the 444-mile-long aqueduct. The aqueduct currently uses water pumped from the delta to irrigate corporate farms in the central valley; remaining water is then pumped at great expense some 2,000 feet over the Tehachapi Mountains, cascading down the southern slope into reservoirs which supply households, swimming pools, and golf courses in Los Angeles and San Diego.

The cities in the southwestern corner of California account for just over half of the state's 23 million people but occupy virtual desert land. These regions and the $13 billion-a-year agricultural section in the valley could not function without massive water subsidies from the north. Because 70 percent of the state's water comes from streams originating in precipitation-rich northern mountain ranges, California is absolutely dependent on gigantic man-made systems for water storage and transport, and California's water politics have given rise to a vicious north-south confrontation. The central questions are: How long can or should the northern part of the state subsidize the exponential growth of the southern portion with water subsidies and should the taxpayers all over the state be forced to shoulder the additional burdens imposed by water greed in the south?

The biggest controversy surrounding the Peripheral Canal, in addition to the enormous present and continuing costs which would be incurred, centered around the prospect of massive environmental damage which could result in the delta from implementation of the plan.[4] The 1,000-square-mile delta, a range of islands and channels which comprises the largest inland river estuary in the continental United States, is rich in bird life and a major spawning ground for striped bass, king salmon, and other fish. Its rich farmlands produce several hundred millions of dollars of vegetable crops each year.

Environmentalists argued that the project would not return adequate water to the delta at "critical points," that is, when river flow is low, particularly during high tides when Pacific Ocean water often intrudes some 80 miles inland. Without adequate infusions of fresh water, the estuary and all life dependent on the delicate salinity balance found there would perish. At stake are not just fish and birds, but the entire ecological balance of a huge region.

There is evidence that the environmentalists are correct in their appraisal of the situation. The currently existing state and federal water pumping stations at the delta's southern edge have been implicated in the recent 60 percent decline and loss in salmon populations. They create a north-south pull which confuses fish during spawning, and millions of fry and eggs are destroyed by the pumps as well.

Even more serious is the saline damage that already results when current pumping operations draw delta water down during low summer flow and allow Pacific tides to push inland. Further drawdowns prompted by the Peripheral Canal would undoubtedly exacerbate these problems.

The controversy has recently come to full fruition. On November 4, 1980, California voters enacted a state constitutional amendment, known as Proposition 8, which was designed to protect the interests of northern Californians following construction of the Peripheral Canal. Only a majority vote of the electorate has temporarily prevented expansion of the State Water Project. But the controversy is far from over.

The Oklahoma Comprehensive Water Plan

As noted earlier, regional water planning is essential if we are to deal effectively with water resource crises. Successful water plans must not eschew technology, but rather must recognize that single-solution alternatives to water problem solving will not work. For example, water diversion may well be a viable alternative, but only if such plans are designed for long-term benefits, are cognizant of potential environmental problems, and recognize that efficient water utilization, the antithesis of uncontrolled demophoric expansion, is an essential component of water resource planning. That is, a realistic regional water plan must maximize both the availability and recharge rates of extant supplies, must be flexible enough to allow for adjustments decades in the future when conditions may change, must be both economically and environmentally sound, and must ensure that real water-demand reductions be implicit in any new populational, industrial, or agricultural expansion projected in the region's future.

Such comprehensive, realistic plans are now being formulated in states where acute and chronic water supply problems have long been commmonplace. One of the most instructive of these examples is the Oklahoma Comprehensive Water Plan.[5]

The state of Oklahoma and the Dust Bowl have become synonymous in recent decades. Reference has been made to the enormous difficulties the High Plains region faces as the Ogallala aquifer is depleted. Without workable water planning, the states of the High Plains will be unable to simultaneously develop critically needed energy reserves while maintaining agricultural productivity.

Oklahoma, like most southern states, is currently experiencing population and industrial expansion. A major oil- and gas-producing state with an important agricultural base, Oklahoma is located in an ecotone, the environmental sensitivity of which was graphically illustrated in the Dust Bowl of the 1930s.

Most of the state's water resources are located in eastern Oklahoma, where abundant rainfall and runoff provide excellent potential for water resource development. An estimated 34 million acre-feet of water currently flow unused out of eastern Oklahoma, into Arkansas and Louisiana, and ultimately to the Gulf of Mexico, an amount far in excess of any projected demands.

In contrast, central Oklahoma, which possesses the resources amenable to large-scale industrial and population expansion, is approaching its environmental carrying capacity in terms of available water. Similarly, western Oklahoma, long a site of fertile irrigated agriculture, will soon be required to supplement or replace the depleted groundwater resources currently used to irrigate fields. In some areas, particularly those relying on the rapidly depleting Ogallala aquifer, irrigation water from groundwater will become impractical within this century.

The Oklahoma Comprehensive Water Plan was formulated for a rapidly growing state in an area inordinately prone to water crises. Nonetheless, the preceding discussion should be ample evidence that no region of the United States will be immune from water problems in the future. Aspects of the Oklahoma plan are undoubtedly subject to criticism, but the idea that water resources must be managed in a comprehensive manner, and in tune with long-range goals, is an important step forward.

In 1957, the Oklahoma legislature created the Oklahoma Water Resource Board, a water authority separate and distinct from other agencies, empowered to direct long-term water resource planning. This board and water resource boards created in other states had limited power until the U.S. Congress passed the Water Resource Planning Act in 1965. This legislation provided the necessary link between federal and state level water planning agencies, allowing comprehensive regional planning to occur.

In 1974, the Oklahoma Senate gave specific statutory authority to the Oklahoma Water Resources Board to prepare a comprehensive state water plan, designed to meet foreseeable contingencies through the year 2040. The key point of the plan developed over the next several years was not that it involved inputs from all levels of government and academia, but that these diverse and sometimes conflicting viewpoints were resolved and dealt with, so that the resulting plan was not only economically viable but environmentally sound. We have seen that the inability of various agencies and individuals to reach a consensus in dealing with water resource problems is one of the major stumbling blocks preventing viable resource planning.

The major problem facing the board was that a realistic water plan had to deal with the asymmetrical distribution of water resources and water demand in the state, while promoting stable economic and population growth well into the next century. The plan had to be flexible enough to allow for adjustments decades in the future when conditions could change, especially those involving actual water resupply patterns. In order for any water strategy developed to be economically and environmentally sound, it had to make maximum use of all readily accessible water supplies, while simultaneously ensuring that water demand reductions be implicit in any new industrial, population, or agricultural expansion. The major thrust, then, had to be a realistic strategy, cognizant of unavoidable, built-in increases in demand for water and of equally unavoidable growth brought on by population and industrial immigration, but insistent that uncontrolled consumption of water and degradation of the environment had to cease.

The results of the board's study were published in 1980. Exhaustive scientific studies of extant water resources and the development potentials of all local sources revealed that, even with stringent conservation, the central and western regions of the state would inevitably experience chronic water shortfalls in the future. These regions had to begin relying on other areas of the state to provide additional water supplies. A number of possibilities were explored, but both state and federal studies indicated that the only viable means of providing additional water to these water-deficient areas appeared to be the transfer of surplus water from eastern Oklahoma, combined with stringent, mandated efforts toward water conservation. Hence, two water conveyance systems were proposed as integral parts of the Oklahoma Comprehensive Water Plan.

This proposed statewide conveyance system would consist of a northern system for the Arkansas River basin and a southern system for the Red River basin. The cost of the northern conveyance system was projected at $5.3 billion (1978 figures), and for the southern conveyance system, $2.5 billion. At ultimate development an annual 1.2 million and 1.3 million acre-feet would be transferred through the northern and southern systems, respectively, for municipal, industrial, and agricultural purposes.

Eleven existing reservoirs were included in both proposed systems to maximize the use of existing projects. A total of twelve proposed and two authorized reservoirs would be constructed as part of the conveyance systems. The northern and southern systems would be 630 miles and 500 miles in length, respectively, and over nine hundred thousand new acres of farmland would be irrigated by these systems. It has been proposed that more than $25 million dollars annually in direct benefits would accrue from increased supplies of irrigation water derived from accessible surface reservoirs rather than depleted groundwater reserves.

However, even though the proposed systems would be independent and built in stages over several decades in order to minimize investment costs, neither system's irrigational component is economically justifiable under current federal guidelines, which assess only direct, primary costs and benefits. Estimates place the cost of irrigation water provided by these conveyance systems at $200 per acre-foot in the southern system and $335 in the northern system. Alternately, the total average value of water conveyed by these systems, if industrial and municipal uses are included, would average $100 per acre-foot in the southern system and $500 per acre-foot in the northern system. Combined municipal, industrial, and agricultural uses generate projected annual direct benefits of approximately $122 million.

To implement the total Oklahoma Comprehensive Plan, including the cost of construction and maintenance of the conveyance systems, would cost about $14 billion over the next several decades. Even with this expenditure, the time required to complete these enormous projects would ensure that chronic spot shortages of water will occur in central and western Oklahoma during the rest of this century. Financing of a project of this magnitude would require the joint efforts of federal, state, local, and private sources.

In view of the costs involved, is Oklahoma justified in proposing such a strategy? One can perhaps best answer that question by considering what would happen, realistically, if such long-term plans are not made and carried out. Irrigation in an area of the country which produces about 10 percent of all the food grown in the United States would largely cease. Even if demand were held constant through massive conservation efforts which reduced the per capita water demands of a state population destined to grow in the future, the environment cannot continue to provide enough water to sustain these people. One might ask, if the eastern part of the state is blessed with adequate water, why not put more money into developing increased growth in that region, rather than transporting water to parched regions, thereby encouraging asymmetrical growth? The answer to that question sums up the real dilemmas faced by resource planners. It would cost more in the long run *not* to develop the oil, gas, and agricultural potential of the central and western part of the state than to subsidize the region's water economy. The lesson is clear: *There are no easy choices, only a series of equally difficult and painful alternatives,* when we decide that a region poor in water must, for other pressing reasons, be developed anyway.

As of this writing, the Oklahoma Senate has passed SB 145, which would establish a water fund of between $25 and $50 million for development of water projects at the local level. No monies have yet been appropriated for the proposed water conveyance system.

Other Technological Alternatives

Not all proposed water supply crisis solutions involve structural modifications of the environment. Proposals discussed here involve the acquisition of more water from hitherto inaccessible sources by application of new technologies. However, with the exception of desalination, the preponderance of evidence suggests that these proposals cannot significantly add to our dwindling supplies of fresh water on a national scale without inordinate expense or environmental damage.

Water from Icebergs

In a National Science Foundation–sponsored study, the Rand Corporation found that Antarctic icebergs might comprise both a technically and economically feasible source of fresh water for southern California and the lower Colorado basin.[6] In its report, Rand outlined a scheme in which icebergs collected from the Antarctic's Ross Sea could be cabled together into iceberg "trains," covered with huge sheets of plastic to inhibit evaporation, and pushed by nuclear-powered tugs and prevailing ocean currents more than 6,000 miles to the shoreline of Los Angeles. There, waste heat from electric-generating plants and heat exchanged from ambient seawater could melt the ice.

The iceberg water, which is much less salty than extant Colorado River water, could provide up to 1 million acre-feet of fresh water to California yearly, supplementing the 1.2 million acre-feet per year drawn from the Colorado by the Colorado River Aqueduct. Rand projected that southern California could one day become a net water exporter, with the Colorado River aqueduct reversed to carry iceberg water to the lower Colorado basin.[7]

The major problem with this proposal is in the energy costs required to transport, convert, and deliver iceberg water to sites of need. Rand put this figure at about $30 per acre-foot; fairly expensive, but still viable. However, in the years since 1973, when the study was completed, energy costs have more than quadrupled, making iceberg water extremely expensive, although still comparable to water costs incurred in structurally based diversion plans such as the Oklahoma Water Plan discussed earlier in this chapter. No studies have been conducted to assess the environmental impact of hauling and melting massive icebergs in the environs of Los Angeles.

Desalination

In the past thirty years, much research has been directed at desalination as a means of augmenting American freshwater reserves. These processes are designed to remove salts and other suspended and dissolved materials from unpotable brackish or saline water, thereby producing potable fresh water. Through evaporative processes, reverse osmosis, and other techniques, we have long had the technological capacity to tap seawater, saline groundwater aquifers, and other hitherto unusable sources to supplant extant freshwater sources. However, several problems have inhibited the large-scale application of desalination technologies. Chief among these problems are the large energy costs inherent in the desalination process and the disposal of brine wastes which accompany water processing.[8]

Improvements in techniques and hardware have lowered the absolute amount of energy required to desalinize salt water. Still, using conventional electric energy sources, desalinized water remains expensive (about $300 per acre-foot). As the cost of conventional energy escalates, so too would the cost of producing fresh water from sea water. Today's price for desalted water generally rules out its use for irrigation and industry, but several communities have demonstrated that in certain coastal areas, the cost is acceptable for high-quality residential water production. For example, desalination produces much of the fresh water used by Key West, Florida, where the costs of piping water from the mainland are extremely high.

One interesting development may brighten the future of large-scale desalination plants, especially in coastal regions of America's Sun Belt. A solar-powered desalination plant capable of producing one thousand gallons per day of fresh water through reverse osmosis of sea water has recently been constructed near Jeddah, Saudi Arabia.[9] While operating costs are not presently available, officials estimate that the solar plant will use about one-half the total energy of conventional thermal plants. The small capacity of this solar plant suggests only that it may serve as a model for larger plants. Clearly, much information and money will be required before solar desalination represents a viable, large-scale alternative water source. Nonetheless, it would seem unwise to rule out such technologies and, like other aspects of solar energy research, we should make every possible effort to determine the feasibility of such water plants.

As noted, the environmental problems associated with the disposal of brine waste are important and sometimes difficult to deal with. For each million gallons of fresh water produced, a desalination plant produces about 2,000 tons of brine waste. For sea water conversion plants ocean discharge of brine is sometimes acceptable, but the waste disposal problems of inland plants are more complex. Possible inland disposal methods include evaporation ponds, transport by pipeline, deep well injection and central stockpiling of dry salts. The estimated monetary costs and environmental impacts of such techniques have not been adequately assessed. Proper disposal costs must be included in any estimates of cost-benefit to justify the construction of desalination plants.

The potential contamination of fresh groundwater and surface water sources by brine wastes and the potential detrimental effects to biota represent real dangers inherent in such technologies.

Despite the many technical and economic problems confronting widespread application of saline water conversion, there appears to be interest in this approach to alleviate water problems in water-poor areas. In February of 1980, *Chemical and Engineering News* reported a forecast which saw the total U.S. desalination capacity approaching 30 billion gallons per day by the year 2000.[10] Approximately one-third of the capacity would be derived from the large-scale desalination plant currently under construction near Yuma, Arizona (see earlier discussion of the Central Arizona Project). The current U.S. desalination capacity, for means of comparison, is about 100 million gallons per day.

Other forecasters are optimistic about the future of desalination because they see a shift from interest in large-scale sea water facilities to smaller, low-energy units for local applications. For example, water requirements for energy resources development could be met by saline waters, appropriately treated and derived from brackish and saline groundwater sources inland. While the cost for pumping water from such formations would be high because many brackish and saline aquifers are located deep within the earth (an example is the Madison formation, a saline aquifer some 1,500 feet deep which underlies much of the freshwater Ogallala aquifer), it would seem advisable to use these waters whenever possible to preserve scarce high-quality water for other uses.

Weather Modification

Weather modification, commonly known as cloud seeding, has received the greatest share of the Federal Bureau of Reclamation's research and development budget.[11] At the request of Congress, studies were initiated in 1961 to document the feasibility of dumping silver iodide from airplanes into clouds to induce rain.

A bureau study estimated that full-fledged cloud seeding could increase the average annual water supply in arid river basins by the following amounts:

- Upper Colorado River basin: 903,000 to 1.3 million acre-feet
- Gila River basin: 154,000 to 239,000 acre-feet
- San Joaquin River basin: 1.2 to 1.5 million acre-feet

The bureau remains skeptical about its weather modification programs (Project Skywalker), emphasizing that they are still in preliminary stages. As well they should be. As we have seen, it is impossible to change the hydrological cycle of a given region without altering the cycling of water in other regions. Evidence also exists which suggests that the existing concentrations of suspended particulate matter and aerosols in our atmosphere, produced from soil erosion, volcanic eruptions, and the industrial activities of man, are sufficiently great to inhibit attempts at cloud seeding.[12]

An excellent summary of the early history and present state of cloud seeding research has recently been published.[13] More than thirty countries are currently involved in weather modification research of some kind. The evidence indicates that seeding convective clouds to increase rainfall is indeed possible but data are not conclusive that this method increases total rainfall. Despite these data, several states, including the Dakotas, Texas, and Oklahoma, have laws on the books governing cloud seeding and have been the sites of many field weather modification applications.

Despite the presence of some legal constraints, the question of whether or not cloud seeding reduces precipitation downwind is not settled. Until it is, legal disputes are certain to arise over whether cloud seeding intercepts rainfall that might have fallen elsewhere to the benefit of others.

Clearly, meaningful economic and technical evaluation of these techniques are limited to special, localized cases. Before we can adequately evaluate the overall feasibility of weather modification in augmenting localized water supplies, we need greater knowledge of predictability of man-induced precipitation events and the effect of such events on broad-scale regional climate. For example, cloud seeding was used in an attempt to mollify the severe drought in the New York City area in 1950.[14] Because a large geographical area was affected, claims that cloud seeding increased the rainfall of the environs of New York by four inches over a thirty-one-week period cannot adequately be assessed. Unless these purported increases in rainfall were destined to fall over the ocean, it would seem that someone else's loss was New York's gain.

In all, attempts to tamper with precipitation patterns, a vital driving force in the hydrological cycle, are ill advised at this time and do not represent a reasonable alternative in increasing regional water supplies.

The Importance of Small-Scale Responses to Water Supply and Water Degradation Crises

Earlier, we emphasized the point that water crises result from the overuse and degradation of extant water supplies by all segments of society. Human cultures appear predisposed to developing water limitations for a number of reasons. Interestingly, a similar pattern of dealing with water problems has also developed in earlier cultures facing acute and chronic water crises. In both Victorian London and in late-twentieth-century America, humans have reacted to water crises by developing technological fixes designed to attack only the most acute and politically expedient manifestations of these crises. Technical and structural solutions are very popular because they involve "distributional policies" in which the general public pays for something that benefits specific interests—regional or economic. In these cases, there are specific winners—hence a strong lobby—but no specific losers. Therefore, the opposition to any single distributional policy (such as the water projects discussed in this chapter) is usually weak. Only when potential problems and losses become graphically and forcefully illustrated, as in the case of the Peripheral Canal in California, does opposition to high-technology, capital-intensive water projects become vehement.

The point is that no water redistribution scheme can provide the ultimate solution to water limitation crises in the United States. At best, each strategy would only forestall the advent of more serious crises because the round of new demophoric growth which would inevitably follow a new infusion of water to a given region would quickly absorb ephemeral water supplies. The only real solution to our water problems involves a combination of sound technological and structural applications with nontechnical/nonstructural solutions involving the *way* in which we use water in the United States. These nontechnical/nonstructural approaches are absolutely vital to solution of our water crises; without them, we will forever be doomed to an endless cycle of boom and bust, until the ultimate environmental carrying capacity of the United States finally becomes exceeded.

The seemingly endless supply of inexpensive water which has fueled the demophoric growth of the United States has effectively been exhausted. Water supplies which do exist and those which could reasonably be developed further can only be acquired through great expense. The logical solution to the intense water problems which plague the United States and which, unless dealt with, will only become infinitely more serious in the years ahead, is that each of us, at all levels of society and in all our activities, must treat liquid water as a highly valued commodity, perhaps the most precious resource in our lives. Continued disregard for the inescapable fact that liquid water supplies cannot be developed infinitely, especially in regions of the country ill suited for massive water subsidy, will precipitate a water crisis of immense proportions which would devastate the American economy. The Water Resources Research Review Committee, acting on the Water Research and Development Act of 1978, has echoed these sentiments in stating: "Sound future water resources management will depend, in part, on answering hard, often unpopular questions about prevailing water use patterns and reallocation possibilities."[15] Let us now look at some of the nonstructural and small-scale structural/technological changes which can be made at all levels of society to effect real and permanent improvements in our water economy.

NOTES

1. *The Issue of the '80's,* Review and Outlook Editorial, *Wall Street Journal,* April 26, 1982, p. 20.

2. J. Boslough, "Rationing of a River," *Science* 81 (1981):26–37; J. Adler et al., "The Browning of America," *Newsweek,* February 23, 1981, p. 36.

3. V. Kayfetz, "California's Water Conflict: North vs. South," *Ambio* 9, no. 6 (1980):319–20; Boslough, "Rationing of a River," p. 36; D. Sheridan, "The Underwatered West: Overdrawn at the Well," *Environment* 23, no. 2 (1981):10–12; Adler, "The Browning of America," pp. 36–37.

4. D. E. Stevens and H. K. Chadwick, "Sacramento–San Joaquin Estuary—Biology and Hydrology," *Fisheries* 4, no. 4 (1979):2–6; Sheridan, "The Underwatered West," p. 12.

5. Oklahoma Water Resources Board, *Oklahoma Comprehensive Water Plan,* Publication 94, April 1, 1980.

6. J. L. Hult and N. C. Ostrander, "Antarctic Icebergs as a Global Fresh Water Resource," Report prepared for the National Science Foundation (Santa Monica, Calif.: Rand Corporation, 1973).

7. Hult and Ostrander, "Antarctic Icebergs," pp. v–26.

8. Sheridan, "The Underwatered West," p. 13; Bureau of Reclamation, *Reclamation Research in the Seventies,* 0–219–743 (Washington, D.C.: U.S. Government Printing Office, 1977), p. 13; W. Viessman, Jr. and C. DeMoncada, *State and National Water Use Trends to the Year 2000,* a report prepared by the Congressional Research Service for the U.S. Senate, Serial No. 96–12 (Washington, D.C.: U.S. Government Printing Office, 1980), pp. 286–88.

9. "Sun Powers Plant to Take Fresh Water from the Sea," *Public Works* 113, no. 2 (1982):74.

10. Viessman and DeMoncada, "State and National Water Use Trends," p. 288.

11. *Reclamation Research in the Seventies,* p. 13.

12. O. B. Toon and J. B. Pollack, "Volcanoes and Climate," *Natural History* 86, no. 1 (1977):8–26; J. M. Prospero, "Dust from the Sahara," *Natural History* 88, no. 5 (1978):55–61; R. A. Bryson, "Ancient Climes on the Great Plains," *Natural History* 89, no. 6 (1979):65–73. Silver iodide added to clouds forms particulate nuclei around which water droplets can coalesce. Current evidence exists that the concentration of potential water droplets forming nuclei in most cloud formations above the United States is generally so high that addition of silver iodide could actually inhibit rainfall. As the desertification of the earth continues, especially in the Sahara of Africa, scientists are finding that the dust content of the atmosphere is increasing. Of course, airborne contaminants also originate from man's activities and from sporadic volcanic eruptions, both of which may profoundly influence global climate and therefore the hydrological cycle.

13. The entire volume 13 of the *Journal of Weather Modification* (1981) is devoted to the history and current status of weather modification projects and represents excellent reading for those interested in this subject.

14. W. E. Howell, "The Precipitation Stimulation Project of the City of New York, 1950," *Journal of Weather Modification* 13 (1981):89–107.

15. *Water Resources,* Newsreport 31, no. 8, published by the National Academy of Sciences, August, 1981, p. 8.

8 What Must Change

The man that makes character makes foes.

E. Young

Aside from the obvious economic and political problems, large-scale technological/structural approaches to water supply crises ignore a major constraint fundamental to a real, permanent solution to our nation's water problems. No water redistribution scheme, however expensive or well conceived, can create more available water; it can only redistribute extant supplies from regions of relative abundance to relative scarcity. There is no question that the heightened availability of water in a hitherto parched region would infuse that region with a degree of heightened productivity. There is also no question about the fact that these benefits would only accrue in the short term. Inevitably, the newly available water would be used to fuel a new round of demophoric growth which would quickly absorb temporary surpluses and lead to a new round of water crises.[1] The severity of this future water crisis would dwarf our current situation, because the overexpanded steady-state economy fostered by the rapid infusion of water could not be sustained without massive water subsidies, which would largely cease to exist. We must realize that *there are finite limits to the amount of water* *which can be extracted from a given environment and that no technology can increase this extractive capacity indefinitely.* These ultimate limits are dictated by events in the hydrological cycle which are beyond man's control. Despite allegations to the contrary, we can do little to increase the amount of precipitation falling on the North American continent, and this would be the only process by which the *absolute* rate of water recharge could be affected. There is, in fact, evidence which suggests that the absolute resupply rate may diminish in coming years due to general climatic drying. However, there is much we can do to maximize the processes which operate in nature to convert rainfall

115

to long-term water storage, and thereby affect the *realized* rate of water recharge.

It is in this vein that meaningful, long-term solutions to our current water crises must develop. We must learn to use water to its maximum potential and foster policies, whenever possible and at all levels of society, which maximize rather than deter the operation of the hydrological cycle. This ethic is beginning to become part of official government policy and must become universally accepted if we are to permanently effect real change.[2]

There are many things we as individuals and as a society can do to ensure a stable transition into what will almost surely be a water-limited future America. We must recognize the fragility and real economic value of the natural processes which supply us with usable water. This "real value" economic view must permeate all water-based industrial, agricultural, and residential practices. Almost every human activity is predicated on the availability of water. This real value is incorporated into every product we produce and use. Any change in policy which requires capital outlay to initiate must reflect this real water cost. Ultimately, these costs must be borne by the consumer. As we directly or indirectly subsidize energy conservation and the development of alternate energy sources, so too must real water costs be reckoned with. In the long run, the notion that water has real economic value will do much to forestall wasteful practices, on both an individual and a collective level. Efficient use and intensive recycling will not cost more in the long run. Rather, the costs will be less, because as fresh water becomes limiting, costs will increase exponentially until excessive use is prohibitive.

By purely voluntary means, without sacrificing individual freedoms or real economic growth, we still can dictate our own water future. Literally, the only factor in the water consumption equation which we cannot change is essential physiological need. We have seen that this amount of water usage is trivial. The thousands of gallons of water used per capita per day by other processes are directly addressable and amenable to change. All changes we propose here not only make good environmental sense, but are also economically beneficial in the real sense of the word. They are predicated as the belief that water is a precious, limiting resource with definite intrinsic value and that this value will increase in the years ahead. Many of these changes sound trivial: they are not. Massive per capita reductions in water usage and environmental constraints which maximize water recharge will occur only through the combined efforts, large and small, of all levels of society.

Residential Changes

Most residential water systems are designed for highly inefficient water use. An average family of four uses approximately 233 gallons of water each day, with 74 percent of that usage occurring in the bathroom.[3] Toilets consume more water than any other fixture in the home, an estimated 40 percent of all water used indoors. Older toilets use 5 to 7 gallons of water per flush. New low-flush toilets or modifications of older models reduce this usage to about 3½ gallons. Technology already exists to adequately flush toilets with less than ½ gallon of water.

Bathing accounts for 34 percent of water used in the home, with about 60 percent of this total used in the shower. Conventional showers use up to 10 gallons per minute. Water use in showers can be reduced up to 70 percent by the installation of inexpensive and readily available water-saving shower heads.

Major kitchen appliances, such as automatic dishwashers and garbage disposals, can be notoriously water-inefficient. Older dishwasher models consume 13 to 16 gallons per cycle; newer water-saving models consume only half as much water per cycle. Water used in hand-washing of dishes can be halved simply through the addition of modified faucets in the kitchen sink.

Other water conservation methods in the home are manifold. These include clothes and dish washing using only full loads, taking shorter showers, using less bath water, and reducing the use of garbage disposals. Outdoors, especially in urban areas, careful discretion in lawn watering can save enormous quantities of water and decrease the runoff of nutrients and pollutants from lawns to stream and groundwater systems. Heavier, less frequent watering during the coolest part of the day minimizes evapotranspiration losses and encourages the development of healthy, deep-rooted grass plants.

We already encourage water conservation in many parts of the country during periodic drought conditions. The general application of water-efficient practices by individuals in the home would go a long way toward alleviating chronic water shortfalls certain to occur in future

United States society. Although residential water use constitutes a relatively minor proportion of total per capita consumption, home water conservation is an important step in changing public attitudes about the preciousness of water. When these attitudes become ingrained, other conservative practices in society as a whole will be more easily accepted. We have seen this pattern already with regard to home energy conservation, and, as in energy limitations, realistic pricing strategies for residential water use may force more stringent residential water conservation.

Water used for residential waste removal is still relatively uncontaminated. To use five gallons of water to dilute one pint of urine is patently absurd. This water can be purified and recycled within the home by systems already developed and on the market. Further, the whole problem of wastewater can be eliminated through waterless sanitary systems currently on the market. In many areas, these systems are presently banned by archaic attitudes and statutes. These laws should be rescinded. To be sure, retrofitting homes for water efficiency, just as for energy efficiency, costs money. Residential tax credits, similar to those extant for energy conservation devices and retrofitting, should be adopted, both on the state and federal levels. In new home construction, a water-efficient system is presently only slightly more expensive than a standard system, and the homeowner would certainly recoup his added investment rapidly as water costs rise precipitously. Further, on-site treatment of wastes and reducing residential water usage put less of a burden on strained municipal water and sewage systems. The need to build more of these expensive facilities would be markedly reduced by individual residential efficiency.

A General Accounting Office (GAO) study (1982) examined the reliability and cost-effectiveness of the sixty-five thousand municipal water delivery systems in the United States and uncovered some shocking statistics.[4] A total of 43 percent of our nation's water delivery systems failed to meet current EPA standards for water purity. While the safety record of the municipal water industry has been remarkably good, 22 deaths and 407 disease outbreaks were directly attributable to unclean drinking water in the period from 1961 to 1978. The GAO estimated that perhaps ten times as many cases were unreported during that same time period.

Additionally, the GAO found that 40 percent of communities surveyed were not charging users enough to cover the costs of delivering water, intending for federal monies to make up shortfalls. Under the present economy realities of federal and state governments, it is unlikely that such pricing strategies will go unchallenged. It is clear that the real costs for residential water use must be reflected in water bills. In a study on residential water use in Tucson during the 1970s, data indicated that higher prices for peak water usage and not appeals for voluntary conservation were the main causal factors for declines in water consumption. In an age where water rights are worth more than land itself in some parts of the U.S. (Colorado is an example) and where water-based mutual funds are seriously being considered, pricing strategies must clearly indicate to consumers that water they use indiscriminantly is dearly bought and precious. New residential construction must also be completed with a realization that water planning is at least as important as energy efficiency.

There is evidence that such planning can work and is economically justified. An ecologically planned community (The Woodlands, Texas) has adopted a unique water management plan designed to avoid adverse water quality effects due to urbanization while maximizing natural existing drainage patterns. An extensive scientific study on this community has documented the plausibility and desirability of such approaches.[5] In addition to wide use of natural buffer areas in construction, this community experimented with a new kind of porous pavement which would permit water infiltration rather than promote runoff of storm waters from nonporous paved surfaces.

Protection of Natural Water Sources

We have emphasized the interrelated nature of groundwater and surface water sources. We have also shown how the hydrological cycle includes a complex web of interactions between terrestrial and aquatic ecosystems. It should be clear by now that the protection of water sources from contamination or excessive water drawdown is an important facet in preserving such sources for continued use by man.[6]

The Safe Drinking Water Act of 1974 recognized the importance of source protection in maintaining and enhancing not only drinking water quality but also the actual supply of usable water for other purposes. Because pollutants rapidly become dispersed in the environment (see chap. 2), it is economically more efficient to keep water sources as pure as possible, so that treatment of water from these sources can produce safe water at reasonable costs.

In chapters 2 and 4, we saw how groundwater and surface water sources become contaminated by toxic wastes, runoff pollutants, and hazardous materials. Erosion and sedimentation, contamination of the atmosphere, and other processes also directly affect the integrity of usable water sources.

The protection of water sources in future America need not resemble the doctrine of protectionism which influenced U.S. environmental policy earlier in its history (see chap. 5). Cognizant of the demands of economic growth and increasing urbanization, a policy of isolation of natural resources is untenable.

Rather, as a nation, we have begun to see the immense economic and health problems which accrue to an entire region when one private company, municipality, or other social unit indiscriminately pollutes a common water source. Legislation to combat the illegal dumping of toxic wastes, the unauthorized use of herbicides, pesticides, and other contaminants within watersheds, the indiscriminant dumping of untreated sludges, and similar violations, already exist. In no case should government agencies become lax in enforcing these laws or rescind them under the guise of economic freedom.

Several "principles of protection" summarize these views:

1. The contamination, pollution, and any degradation of the quality of water supply sources have damaging effects on health, well-being, *and economy,* as well as on the general environment.
2. Physical laws dictate that dispersed pollutants are *always* more expensive and difficult to clean up. From an economic standpoint, cleanup efforts must be directed as close to the source of contamination as possible.
3. The responsibility for preventing and abating pollution or contamination of water sources rests with those who discharge noxious materials, directly or indirectly, into water sources, the land environment, or the atmosphere.
4. Because water problems are generally regional in nature, all levels of government and industry must coordinate and accept the responsibility for water source protection.

5. Land, water, and air are interrelated resources. Planning, management, and use of these common resources must consider their mutual influences and impacts in an integrated manner.[7]

We spoke earlier about the usefulness of natural buffer areas to increase water recharge rates, decrease erosion, and ameliorate the effects of waterborne pollutants. The protection of water sources must include inland wetland areas. There are many concrete examples linking the degradation of wetlands to the disruption of other water sources. The Everglades of Florida, which represents a vast network of wetlands, is essential not only for the preservation of countless plant and animal species, but also to the water economy of the state of Florida.

While the vast size of the Everglades makes it a particularly graphic example of these processes, similar effects can be noted in most marsh habitats. For example, one of the major problems associated with reservoir impoundments, particularly in regions like Tennessee, the plains, and the Southwest where erosional loss of soils is high, is that sedimentation processes rapidly fill the newly constructed reservoirs with silt, fouling the waters and reducing the useful life of the reservoir. Thus, a body of water with a projected life of perhaps a hundred years must be dredged every few years at great expense or else will fill within decades. Researchers have demonstrated that the lack of marsh vegetation surrounding the margin of many of these systems is an important contribution to high sedimentation rates.[8] The marsh habitat stabilizes soils which would otherwise wash into the water body. In an age where new construction of reservoir systems is becoming increasingly expensive, the economic benefits of so simple a strategy as wetland protection readily becomes apparent.

Agricultural Water Use and Degradation

Agricultural water use exceeds nearly every other component of the water utilization equation. Poor agricultural techniques contribute large quantities of pollutants to surface water systems and reduce the percolation of rainfall so necessary to groundwater recharge. The projected increased demand for food makes it imperative that irrigation water conservation and wise land use practices supplant currently prevalent methods.

It is clear that massive supplies of cheap irrigation water may cease to exist in much of the United States. Further, intensive irrigation and resultant salination of once fertile soils has become an expensive and increasingly alarming problem. We presently have the technological capacity to address these problems. The time has come to implement these changes.

Farmers are increasingly moving away from wasteful irrigation processes, but this trend must become more widespread. Since 85 percent of the freshwater demand on a world level is consumed by agricultural irrigation, conservation in this area has enormous economic and environmental impact. We know that most irrigation water is wasted through improper or excessive application. It is against this background that trickle or drip irrigation is gaining increasing acceptance. Drip irrigation, in which the crop, not the soil, is irrigated, has been in use for nearly fifty years, but has only recently become widely applied. In drip irrigation, water is applied slowly and uniformly to a crop at or below soil level and adjacent to the plant by means of mechanical water outlets.

Water uptake by plants is more efficient and far less soil water is lost through evaporation as compared to conventional methods like center-pivot irrigation. In arid regions such as Israel, nearly all irrigated land is moistened by the drip method. Recently, California, Texas, Florida, Arizona, Michigan, and Hawaii have begun to supplant older methods with modified drip irrigation techniques. In Israel, water for irrigation is used with 85 to 90 percent efficiency compared with only 35 to 40 percent efficiency for the United States as a whole.[9]

In addition to actual water savings, drip irrigation has many other economic benefits. Labor and energy costs for pumping are reduced greatly, so much so that the typical drip system can often pay for itself within one year of operation. Weed growth is retarded since only the areas immediately adjacent to the crop are watered. Drip irrigation can use water of higher salinity than conventional techniques. In the drip method, accumulated salts are pushed to the periphery of the wetted soil by the advancing front of water. Since the total water added to the soil is much less than with conventional methods, the overall salination of the soil is similarly reduced.

Problems in drip irrigation do exist. There is a tendency for soils to become salinized over a long period of time unless a small amount of deep percolation is allowed from time to time to leach salts below the rooting zone. Water must be filtered prior to application so that the emitters are not clogged by particles. In marginal agricultural areas, however, more crop yield can be grown on far less water and for far less money than by any conventional technique.

Trickle or drip irrigation is by no means the only way to reduce our vast irrigation water subsidies without harming crop yields. If we look at the 97 million acre-feet of water consumed by irrigated agriculture on an annual basis in the United States (1975 figures), the potential for massive water savings immediately becomes evident. In 1979, a governmental interagency report by the Departments of the Interior and Agriculture and the U.S. Environmental Protection Agency determined that additional public and private investment of up to $5 billion over the next three decades directed at water conservation in irrigated agriculture could decrease gross annual diversions of irrigation water by 15 to 20 million acre-feet *using existing technology*.[10]

What are some of these suggested strategies? First, we must realize that any irrigational strategy must be tailored to local and regional conditions. The regional diversity of climatic regimes, soil conditions, and water demands in the United States is vast. The irrigation needs, economies, and water resources of each region of the country differ greatly. We have seen that the heterogeneous nature of water supply and demand in the continental United States creates many problems for resource planners. Nonetheless, regional similarities in irrigation requirements do exist, and allow planners to simplify strategies somewhat.

The continental United States can be conveniently segregated into a series of irrigation characterization areas based on regional similarities in annual rainfall and runoff, topography, soil conditions, crops, and other factors (fig. 3). We have already discussed some of these regional similarities in earlier treatments of freshwater dynamics and regional water crises. Despite small local differences, growers in a given area, e.g., the southwestern region, can be expected to encounter similar irrigational needs and problems and would benefit by similar strategies to meet these needs. In spite of the diverse nature of these regions, certain conservative practices have universal appeal. In the next section, we will discuss the enormous savings of water which would accrue from more general use of wastewater effluents in irrigation. For now, we will look at strategies designed to increase the efficiency of water delivery to crops, from wherever that water comes. Such strategies become pro-

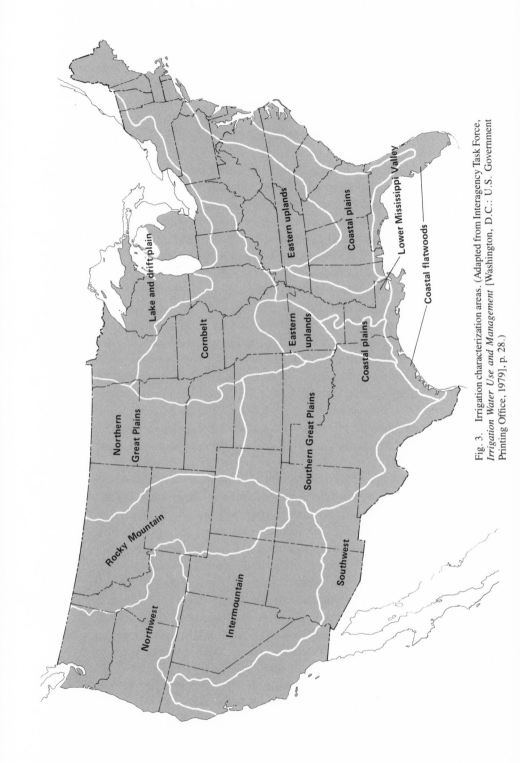

Fig. 3. Irrigation characterization areas. (Adapted from Interagency Task Force, *Irrigation Water Use and Management* [Washington, D.C.: U.S. Government Printing Office, 1979], p. 28.)

gressively more important in regions like the western half of the United States, where water is chronically scarce.

One major way to save water in irrigation is to line irrigation channels and laterals with impermeable materials like concrete or flexible plastic. Lining a conveyance system reduces seepage of valuable water by approximately 75 to 90 percent. Other benefits of lining delivery channels include (1) the control of ditchback weeds and aquatic plants which consume water, (2) a reduction in soil erosion, (3) an improvement in water quality, (4) a reduction in operation and maintenance costs, (5) reduced drainage requirements, and (6) reclamation of agricultural lands lost to seepage. There are, of course, certain drawbacks to lined conveyance systems. They may reduce vegetation and open water habitats used by wildlife and may reduce percolation of water to shallow groundwater reserves.

Piped conveyance systems, generally used to date only in mountainous areas, can increase water delivery efficiencies to greater than 95 percent. In addition, piped systems lose little or no water to evaporation, a major consideration in overall water efficiency.

In each of the above systems, planners have reinforced the need for more stringent control over the rate and timing of water deliveries to irrigators. In the past, unregulated delivery of irrigation water often led to waste and excessive wetting of field crops. A recent federal program has outlined guidelines for water deliveries within local distributional systems that would not only save water but also might lessen the need for construction enlargements of existing delivery systems.

Once water is delivered to the farm, much can be done to ensure its wise use. Field testing of water control structures, land leveling systems, flow measurement devices, and tailwater recovery systems have demonstrated that great water savings are possible on most irrigated land with minimal capital expenditure. For example, while drip irrigation may be impractical for small grain crops such as wheat or sorghum, farmers can easily adapt furrow or sprinkler systems for heightened efficiency. Research has shown that with wheat and sorghum, water can be applied in furrows as far as 160 inches apart (as opposed to the 40-inch furrows normally used) without loss of crop yield.[11] Such wide-furrow irrigation can also be used with center-pivot systems, using drop tubes in the pivot arms instead of sprayers. In effect, more water is made available for plant use; less is wasted to evaporation, percolation, and runoff.

Clearly, the farmer needs help in understanding and applying the complexities of efficient water management to his own situation. The Department of Interior's Bureau of Reclamation provides an Irrigation Management Services program to districts associated with reclamation projects. Several universities, state agencies, irrigation organizations, and numerous private firms provide similar services in planning assistance. Statistics on such programs indicate that 20 percent increases in water use efficiency are easily obtainable. So far such programs have only been applied on about 1 million of the 50 million acres of irrigated farmland in the United States (1977 figures); clearly, much remains to be done.[12]

In the current economic climate of high interest rates and low crop prices, the farmer must not only be convinced that water use efficiency will help him, but he must also receive some sort of governmental help to achieve such goals. There are numerous economic benefits and incentives to improving irrigation efficiency, especially in water-poor regions of the West. As we have noted, reduction in labor requirements, better utilization of fertilizers, energy savings, and higher crop productions all put more money in the pocket of the farmer who improves the efficiency of his irrigation strategy.

To help farmers in this area, most states now have several programs aimed at fostering agricultural water conservation. Because states are generally responsible for administering water laws, water rights, and regulatory programs and because state universities, especially land grant institutions, are heavily committed to agricultural research, such programs can be very useful. Aside from planning assistance, many states have substantial funds available for grant or loan programs, primarily involving construction loan funds which are available at reduced interest rates. Many such programs also use federal dollars and all are designed to improve the efficiency of outdated irrigation systems. It is encouraging that, even in hard economic times, most states are currently expanding, rather than cutting back, funding levels to water programs. This expansion must be accelerated.

Federal programs for irrigation assistance, which began with the passage of the Reclamation Act of 1902, remain a major source of direction in the effort toward agricultural water conservation. Some thirty-five federal programs involving about ten separate agencies are currently involved in irrigation assistance, and in recent years funding levels have exceeded $175 million annually. However, with recent cuts in the budgets of such agencies as the Environmental Protection Agency and with the recent presidential thrust toward a "New Federalism," the federal government cannot be counted on to shoulder the major portion of the burden for water development funding.

Many observers and analysts believe that the private sector is more than capable of picking up the slack in this regard. It is estimated that in 1977, private annual investment in irrigational improvements exceeded $710 million.[13] It seems clear from past experience that federal/state/local/private cost-sharing strategies will offer real benefits to government, individual farmers, and private investors in the decades ahead.

Improvements in irrigation methods are not the only water-saving measures which can be adopted. Most agricultural fields are currently planted in row upon row of monospecific stands. Maintaining an artificial monoculture requires proportionately greater energy and water inputs than growing multiple crops on the same site. Whenever possible, multiple crop planting should supplant monoculture agriculture, particularly in marginal farming areas. Water losses in marginal semiarid areas can also be minimized through plant enclosure techniques, which are particularly useful for vegetable crops.

Much agricultural irrigation water is drawn from groundwater aquifers, even in parts of the country, such as the plains, where groundwater reserves are already overburdened. Pumping water from deep within the earth requires much more energy than is required to pump surface waters. In the interests of both energy and water conservation, surface waters should be used whenever possible for irrigation, thus reserving the frequently higher quality groundwaters for more direct human needs.

The increased development of salt-tolerant plants, so-called halophytes, is another important step in making irrigation water go further and preserving higher grade water for direct human use.[14] The possibilities are tantalizing. Every year, another half-million acres of farmland worldwide become too salty for conventional farming because of saline accretions resulting from evaporating irrigation water. Specifically, 12.7 percent of the agricultural real estate in California and up to one-fourth of the land within the lower Rio Grande Valley have serious salinity problems. While saline soils and irrigation water are incompatible with normal crop growth, halophytes can be cultivated with brackish water containing salinities of over 3,000 parts per million (roughly one-tenth the salinity of ocean water). Approximately one-tenth of the total North American land mass lies directly over reachable, brackish aquifers within this salinity range which could be used in halophyte or drought-resistant plant agriculture. In all, it is believed that the United States has ready access to more than 18.5 billion acre-feet of readily pumpable saline groundwater, including roughly 3 billion acre-feet (roughly the volume of Lake Michigan) in the critically water-short mountainous West.

The general use of high-yield "Green Revolution" strains, which produce high yields only with massive water and energy subsidies, has prevented the widespread development and utilization of drought-resistant and salt-tolerant plant cultures, because until recently, these water and energy subsidies have been available at reasonable cost. As water and energy diminish in availability, we must be ready to replace water-dependent crops with other strains or face agricultural chaos. To this end, research aimed at developing alternate crop strains must intensify and agricultural water subsidy practices, which grant depletion allowances to excessive users of irrigation water, must be phased out. The latter practice only acts to forestall the necessary change to less water-intensive farming practices more in line with economic and environmental realities.

Wastewater Reuse

The American propensity for cleanliness has led to great benefits by reducing disease and permitting diversion of our energies to other activities. That cleanliness can be misconstrued and detrimental if carried to the extreme. The repulsion of many to human waste products is an immature attitude—we must enter a recycling society, and the nutrients of human origin cannot be wasted. The waste products can easily be rendered safe from communicable diseases and are no different from the wastes of other animals. Despite superior intellect, humans are still functionally animals!

Human sewage, rich in valuable plant nutrients, can be pumped directly onto fields with minimal treatment, in effect recycling both water and nutrients. The erroneous idea that this practice is somehow unsanitary must be replaced with an appreciation for the beneficial overall effects of sewage utilization. We can no longer afford to waste either fertilizer, energy, or water in agriculture. It may take a massive informational campaign for such recycling techniques to become acceptable, but the beneficial effects would be well worth it.

According to governmental statistics, more than 50 percent of the wastewater sludges produced by municipalities are disposed of on land.[15] The potential value of wastewater reutilization in both water conservation and the addition of valuable nutrients and organic matter to farmland has only recently been thrust to the forefront. Although certain problems appear to exist in the accumulation of potentially toxic trace metals in crops grown on wastewater-amended fields, the overall beneficial effects are overwhelming.[16] The needs for irrigation water and inorganic fertilizers are strongly curtailed and plant yields increase significantly.

Despite the demonstrated usefulness of liquid wastewater, most municipalities still expend considerable time and energy in the drying of wastewater sludge. Municipal Chicago's West-Southwest Sewage Treatment Works, one of the largest treatment plants in the world, processes in excess of 635 dry metric tons of sludge per day, using at least 67,800 kilowatts of electricity per day in the sludge-drying process.[17] A plan now under consideration would eliminate the sludge-drying process, thereby saving millions of dollars in energy costs and millions of gallons of water every year.

Many field tests have been completed which support the efficiency of land application systems for recycling of wastewater. Several different techniques (spray irrigation, groundwater recharge by rapid infiltration, and overland flow; see fig. 4) have been applied with a large variety of waste materials (agricultural, municipal, and industrial). The U.S. Environmental Protection Agency (EPA) has published a design manual outlining factors to consider and design and evaluation procedures to facilitate wastewater usage.[18]

The city of Tallahassee, Florida, which began wastewater irrigation practices in the 1940s, was recently the site of an EPA study designed to document the effect of wastewater application on crop yields and soil characteristics.[19] Effluent from a secondary treatment plant was applied by spray irrigation to crops grown in fine, sandy soil. Summer crops included coastal bermuda grass, sorghum, millet, corn, and kenaf, while winter crops included rye and ryegrass. Summer irrigation rates were as high as 200 mm (8 inches) of water per week while up to 100 mm (4 inches) of water per week was applied to winter fields. In both summer and winter crops, yields increased with water application rate.

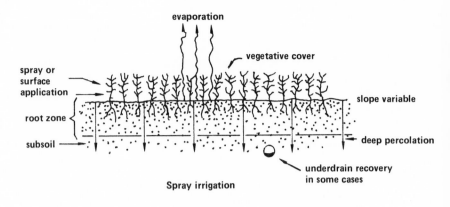

Spray irrigation

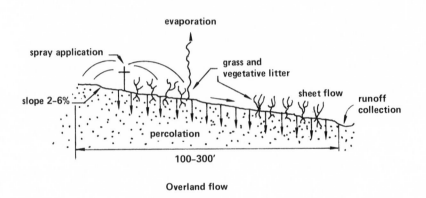

Overland flow

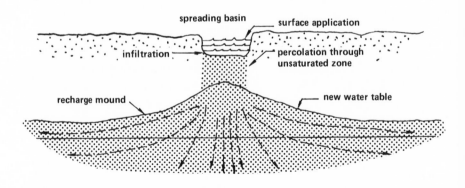

Rapid infiltration

Fig. 4. Examples of methods of land disposal of wastewater. (Adapted from S.C. Reed et al., *Waste Water Management by Disposal on the Land,* Special Report No. 171 [Hanover, N.H.: U.S.A. Cold Regions Research and Engineering Laboratory, 1972].)

The soil was very effective at removing fecal coliform bacteria from the effluent as well as phosphorus, while at high irrigation rates (more than 50 mm per week) some nitrogen percolated into the groundwater. Soil pH remained at around 6.5, in the optimum range for crop production.

In another study near Pauls Valley, Oklahoma, the overland flow method of wastewater application received extensive analysis.[20] Here, municipal wastewater equivalent to approximately one-third the average flow of domestic sewage from Pauls Valley, a community of about six thousand people, was applied to test sites exhibiting slopes of 2 and 3 percent. Each plot was seeded with a variety of grasses. Here again, bacterial numbers, biochemical oxygen demands, viral contaminants, and suspended solids were greatly reduced and infiltration of applied water was rapid.

The long-term effects of applications of domestic wastewater are documented in another EPA investigation.[21] On a test farm near Roswell, New Mexico, slow-rate irrigation of crops by wastewater has been in progress since 1944. Here, effluent flowing through a concrete-lined ditch was channeled to run down furrows in the fields. Analyses of water, soils, and plants at the Roswell site in 1977 indicated that the use of wastewater for irrigation resulted in several long-term benefits. No viruses or fecal coliform bacteria had penetrated the soils and reached underlying groundwater, nor were indicator viruses found either on the surfaces or inside leaf tissue or grain of corn grown on the effluent-irrigated land. Heavy metals such as zinc, copper, and chromium were not being assimilated at a greater rate in effluent-irrigated plants than in similar crops at nearby groundwater-irrigated sites. More toxic heavy metals such as cadmium, lead, and mercury were demonstrably absent from the irrigation effluent, the underlying groundwater, and the irrigated corn crop. Arsenic and selenium concentrations in effluent-treated soils have remained comparable to other soils in the area. In contrast, plant nutrients, nitrogen and phosphorus, have increased in the effluent-irrigated soil by about 50 percent, as contrasted with groundwater-irrigated soils. There was no indication of pesticide or herbicide contamination in effluent-irrigated soils.

This study suggested that the Roswell site could continue to be irrigated by effluent water for another hundred years without harmful effects. Not only did this process return scarce water back to soil and groundwater storage, but the city of Roswell realized an income of over

$11,000 in 1977 from the sale of effluent water to farmers, golf course operators, and other users.

How are wastewater reuse plans implemented in these days of high interest rates? What institutions are involved? In the fledgling Beaver Irrigation District near Lowell, Arkansas, a plan is currently being implemented that would access some of the 1 million gallons per day of backwash water produced in treatment plants in the Beaver Water District of northwest Arkansas.[22] A severe drought in 1980 was a financial blow to all northwest Arkansas farmers, with fruit farmers especially hard hit. Following the 1980 drought, public pressure fostered the formation of the irrigation district, which became a legal entity in May of 1981. Farmers in the area currently pay about $200 per acre-foot of irrigation water and, as one farmer said "the new system should cut that to less than $50. With production costs up 15 to 20 percent and berries up only around 5 percent, any savings we can manage is important" (Stubblefield 1982, p. 7).

Work is underway on putting together a contract with the Beaver Water District under which the irrigation district will pay the water district $100,000 for connection rights. In return, the irrigation district is to receive the wastewater free for twenty years. Eighteen area farmers with about 900 acres of crops are in the irrigation district and there will be enough water to irrigate over 1,000 acres.

Farmers must have storage capacity for half their allotment for the year, about 50 to 60 acre-feet, which would be stored in holding ponds. Construction of 4- and 12-inch plastic distribution lines, buried for protection, will probably start in the late summer of 1982. The costs for holding pond and pipeline construction will be subsidized by state and federal agencies; a $300,000 grant from the state office of the Soil Conservation Service and a $200,000 loan from the Farmers' Home Administration are already approved. An additional $300,000 in matching funds for holding pond construction with the Agricultural Stabilization and Conservation Service is pending.

Farmers see their work as more than just a way to fill a need on their own land. A local farmer who raises blueberries and strawberries in the district said, "This way we can use backwash water for a productive purpose that otherwise would cost additional funds to treat" (Stubblefield 1982, p. 7).

Clearly, the institutional support exists for a broad application of such plans across America. True, we need further research on the long-term effects of wastewater application on soil and climate types found in irrigation areas. But overwhelming evidence exists which says that wastewater reuse is an old idea whose rejuvenation time has come. One need only look at California, where a state report recorded that over 2 million acre-feet of wastewater are produced annually—a massive amount of water which could be used to stave off drought in the Central Valley, the coastal basin, and the San Joaquin basin.[23]

Current agricultural practices also cause other, more direct water resource problems which must be addressed. As noted earlier, agriculture has become the single biggest polluter of two-thirds of the U.S. river basins. Non–point source inputs of nutrients which fuel algal blooms and eroded soils degrade more freshwater supplies than industrial or residential inputs combined. Increasing quantities of toxic pesticides and herbicides now find their way into surface and groundwaters directly from agricultural sources. Unless agriculture-caused water pollution is sharply curtailed, clean water goals ordered by Congress simply cannot be met.

Clearly, these trends must be reduced. Wise land use practices must be returned to America's farmlands. Marginal land should not be used for grain production. Contour plowing must again become the norm. In 1977, Congress created a new Rural Clean Water Program, designed as an innovative effort to help farmers stop both farm-caused water pollution and soil erosion. These policies must become generally adopted. The farmer must realize that he cannot continue unwise practices "just one more year" in a vain effort to recoup past losses. To do so mortgages his future and that of all who depend on him for food and on water downstream from his farm for necessary consumption. Conservative farming techniques, like so many other water-conservative techniques we have already discussed, are cost-effective, both in the short and long runs.

Agriculturists must recognize the importance of buffer areas. Forested, natural growth areas must be retained or, if absent, developed to assist in control of erosion and effective recharge of groundwater aquifers. Intermittent windbreaks not only reduce wind-transported soil movement and losses, but also reduce soil evaporation and plant transpiration rates. Buffer vegetation areas between tilled land and surface waters slow runoff and allow greater time for percolation to groundwater, as well as reducing particulate and nutrient intrusion to surface streams, lakes, and reservoirs. Wetlands can serve as major groundwater recharge sites and should not be drained. The small amount of acreage held in these buffer zones will more than compensate for the short-lived economic gains obtained from total exploitation of every possible acre of land.

Those struggling with the alternatives to wise land use practices might ponder the words of Dr. Priscilla Grew, director of the Department of Conservation of California: "Where soil is lost, civilization also goes with it. Today soil is as essential for the production of food and fiber as it was during the Neolithic."[24] Truly, soil and water problems are interdependent; we cannot solve one without addressing the other. And solve them we must—our societal future depends on it.

Industrial Changes and Governmental Roles

Industrial consumption of water continues to rise every year in our demophorically expanding society. Much industrial water consumption involves one-time use and discarding of intake water for cooling or metal processing. Even in areas where water is relatively abundant, the industrial demand for water is increasing sharply. The Great Lakes Basin Commission estimates that as the human population of the region doubles between 1970 and 2020, the demand for Great Lakes water will increase tenfold, a perfect example of exploding demophoric growth in action.[25] These figures mean that approximately 100 billion gallons of water per day would be withdrawn from the lakes and returned in various stages of degradation. Today, up to 0.1 percent of the inshore waters of the Great Lakes are used every day for power plant cooling purposes. By the year 2000, that daily figure probably will exceed 1 percent in Lake Michigan and 3 percent in Lake Ontario.

The generation of electricity ranks second only to agriculture in withdrawals of water. In 1975, for example, steam electric generation cooling processes accounted for about 37 percent of all freshwater withdrawals in the United States.[26] However, *consumptive* use of water by these power plants amounts to only about 2 percent of the total U.S. consumption. Again, the major problem confronting designers and operators of steam electric generation plants is to increase the efficiency of cooling processes using water, so that less need be withdrawn from stressed freshwater supplies. Many power plants still utilize water withdrawn from surface or groundwater only once and then discharge it, simply because it remains inexpensive to do so. In situations where water is more limited, cooling ponds or cooling towers are often used. When cooling water is very scarce, dry cooling towers may also be used. In these systems, cooling water circulates in a closed system and heat is dissipated with little water loss, much like an automobile radiator. The point is that increased water efficiency in power plant cooling would go a long way toward forestalling water demand crises, particularly in urban areas poorly blessed with water reserves. The National Water Commission has estimated that general adoption of recirculating cooling systems would reduce this major freshwater demand to less than 2 percent of current levels and that higher water prices appear to be the most realistic incentive to foster such retrofitting.[27] The commission and other governmental agencies have recommended that government subsidies for water consumption, a common feature of this and other industries, must be curtailed, since they act as incentives for continued waste by making water artificially cheap. The commission has also emphasized that coastal states should make greater use of saline ocean water for cooling purposes, thus preserving fresh waters for other necessary uses. Florida, for example, has gone increasingly toward saline water cooling in power plants. Yet, many power plants in Florida and other coastal states continue to consume fresh waters for cooling, thus putting unnecessary demands on limited freshwater supplies.

Aside from electric generation, the Water Resources Commission in 1975 noted that manufacturing industries accounted for about 17 percent of the nation's freshwater withdrawal.[28] The commission also found that this water was recycled an average of 2.2 times before being returned to its source. Iron and steel, chemical, pulp and paper, petroleum refining, and food industries are all heavy users of water. The commission further projected that although total water use by manufacturing industries may increase fivefold by 2000, total freshwater and saline withdrawals could actually decrease by about 50 percent compared with 1975 levels if large-scale improvements were made in in-plant water recycling techniques. Clearly, without massive water recycling, manufacturing as a whole could face severe water limitation in the near future.

In addition, technological innovations which save water during the manufacturing process itself demonstrate that great improvements can still be made. For example, 1970 vintage pulp and paper mills employing available, newer technologies use about 62 percent as much water per ton of product as 1960 vintage plants. One avenue available to stimulate industrial water conservation is the strict enforcement of antipollution laws. If industry were forced by legal constraints to release smaller amounts of more highly purified water into the environment, every consideration would be made to limit the amount of water usage in the name of monetary savings. Here again is a perfect example of how stringent environmental regulations can actually benefit the long-term economic climate in the United States by limiting wasteful consumption of scarce resources.

Enlightened industrial concerns are already beginning to realize that it is in their own best interest to conserve water. Industrial co-operatives, consisting of a few plants to over thirty allied industrial concerns, are being set up all across America by private industry and are pooling resources to deal with problems of wastewater treatment and recycling and other water-related problems.[29] Do they work? Industrial managers say yes. Such cooperative schemes spread the costs of dealing with expensive problems to a number of different sources, saving everyone time and money. There are also state-level programs which assist industry with water-use credits, similar to energy credits, which pinpoint places a specific plant can save water. The Oklahoma Industrial Water Management program has estimated that in the past few years they have saved industrial clients some 36 million gallons of water. In a typical audit, water and energy cost savings pay back the price of an audit in less than a year.[30]

By necessity, governmental roles in industrial water conservation must be large. Presently, many industries are leaving the relatively water-rich areas of the Midwest and relocating in the water-poor southern and western regions. This trend is causing disproportionate demand for limited water in the South and West. As we have seen, this migration cannot long continue without fragile water reserves being decimated through competition among people, industry, and agriculture. The government's role in stemming this migratory flood could be considerable and is ultimately in the best interests of the country as a whole. Taxation laws on the local, state, and national level can be rewritten to encourage relocation of industries in areas supplied with adequate water. Taxation and depreciation allowances for new equipment should also reflect the real value of water as a limiting resource, just as we presently allow for energy-efficient retrofitting. Water-intensive practices and relocation of industry in water-poor regions may appear justifiable in the short term, but within several years, the real costs of water could make these factors economically prohibitive. The consumer, government, and industry must soon recognize the cost-benefits of sound water practices.

Fortunately, there is every indication that government and industry *are* recognizing the need for a new view of water conservation in the American economy. The Carter administration in 1978 proposed sweeping changes in governmental roles in the nation's water economy, stressing nonstructural, conservationist methods as the cornerstone of sound water policy.[31] Economic chaos in the intervening years threaten to undermine such work, as a stressed economy seeks to rewrite environmental legislation denounced as fiscally irresponsible. If anything has been stressed in this book so far, it is that *there is no inherent conflict between sound economics and sound resource utilization.* As a nation, we must resist the temptation to relax the vigilant control and supervision of those who would despoil *common* resources for personal gain, for, inevitably, we as consumers eventually pick up the tab. That tab will be many times greater than the cost of effective resource utilization at all stages of use.

But government and industry do not simply have a responsibility to reduce water usage. One of the most pressing acute and chronic water problems we face is the question of toxic waste disposal. We have already discussed the potentially catastrophic effects of toxic waste dumps on both surface and groundwaters, and the degradative effects of airborne contaminants. As we discover more and more of these dump sites and learn more about atmospheric contamination problems like acid rain in the years to come, the scope of the problem will become truly immense.

Only recently have industries responsible for introduction of wastes into the environment been held responsible for their actions. Inevitably, though, the cleanup efforts which have been proposed have been financed directly or indirectly from taxation of individual citizens (a good example is the proposed Three Mile Island cleanup plan currently being formulated). The safe disposal of toxic chemicals and industrial pollutants must become a top priority of industry. Water resources and the atmosphere itself must be recognized as common property and treated as such. One adage from the early environmental movement still holds true—nothing ever "goes away." Toxic waste disposal should become a recognized part of doing business, and, by definition, these costs must be borne by the consumers of products. From an energetic/economic standpoint, cleanup of wastes before they become dispersed in the aquatic, terrestrial, or atmospheric environment is always infinitely cheaper and easier than after-the-fact efforts. We must pay sooner or later. If later, the costs in both economic and human terms are staggering and intolerable.

Another concern must be addressed by industrial consumers of water. Presently, particularly in regions poor in surface waters, groundwater is pumped from deep aquifers, used for industrial purposes, and then released into surface systems. We have seen that groundwater recharge rates are much slower than those of surface systems. To prevent rapid depletion of precious groundwater aquifers, water taken from subsurface aquifers must, after cleanup, be returned to these sources. Furthermore, whether surface or subsurface water is used in industrial processing, the liquid water volume returned to the environment must meet or exceed that volume initially removed from the source. Losses of liquid water through evaporation and runoff can be immense and result in large net losses of water from areas which can ill afford deficits.

Water-conservative practices in industry, as those already discussed in the residential and agricultural fields, are economically beneficial now. They will become even more cost-effective in the future. Clearly, there is no conflict here between what is "good for industry" and what is good for the United States as a whole.

General Water Supply/Resupply Changes

We cannot long take more water from existing supplies than that which comes in through natural recharge processes. As we have seen, there is little we can do about increasing precipitation, a driving force of the hydrological cycle. There is much, however, that we can do to improve the effectiveness of precipitation in recharging surface and groundwater supplies. We can reduce demand for water through conservation, but that may not be enough, particularly if climatic change reduces the potential recharge rate of the nation's water supplies.

One way to increase recharge rates is to increase the amount of time water is in contact with the continental land mass before it flows out to sea. River channelization, which increases the water flow-through rate of river systems, is an unwise practice and should be curtailed sharply. It is argued that channelization reduces the threat of flooding in low-lying areas, but the evidence for this viewpoint is controversial. A critical eye should be directed toward any proposed channelization project. These projects are inconsistent with maximizing water recharge rates.

Many land use practices which decrease recharge rates must be reevaluated and changed. Our national goal should, whenever possible, be to preserve important water retention sites. We are beginning to realize the real economic value of heretofore "useless" wetlands and other natural buffer areas. Clear-cut deforestation, spreading patches of concrete which increase quantities and rates of urban runoff, and the drainage of wetlands are incongruous with the important goal of maximizing our precious water supplies. They simply do not make economic sense any longer, even in the short run.

In every part of the country, water resource problems now and in the future will have their own unique character. In each of these regions, specific benefits and debits should be weighed so that a reasonable, comprehensive regional water policy may be adopted. We have seen that the geopolitical influence of a large urban area far exceeds its geographical boundaries. Such regional water planning makes sense in the ebb and flow of water in the hydrosphere. Whatever policy a particular region adopts, it must maximize water strengths while minimizing demands on weak links in the system. For example, areas which depend almost exclusively on groundwater, particularly those in coastal regions, must rely increasingly on more rapidly replaced surface waters.

Concluding Remarks

How will we as a people respond to chronic water limiting conditions? If we refuse to recognize the problem we are destined to repeat the mistakes of past societies. No one can predict the uncertainties of the future. Anyone who examines the current and projected situation cannot fail, however, to be impressed with the magnitude and importance of water problems in any formula for an increasingly prosperous United States society. No one can fail to ponder the implications for the world situation if the United States can no longer meet its obligations as a net food exporter and world leader. Yet, in hard economic times, like those extant in the early 1980s, we are tempted to reduce spending and commitments of talent to solving problems which, on the face of it, seem not to be economically important. We have stressed over and over the real economic value of usable water to the American society. The mood of government, industry, and the American people is uncertain. The temptation is to return to "business as usual," and abandon progress made on understanding the basic and applied aspects of water research. The temptation is great to relax, rather than strengthen, policies which recognize the common property concept of water resources.

We are faced with a great challenge, one which will dwarf the energy crisis by comparison. For while we can substitute other forms of energy for oil or gas, we cannot substitute techological alternatives for water. Water crises, unlike other crises, develop slowly. Because they are slow to evolve, man classically addresses only their acute and visible manifestations. To prosper in the next century, we must turn away from this notion. We must, in short, become the first advanced techological society in the history of man to directly address his own techological limitations—and the first to progress beyond societal adolescence in a resource-limited biosphere.

NOTES

1. J. R. Vallentyne, "Freshwater Supplies and Pollution: Effects of the Demophoric Explosion on Water and Man," in *The Environmental Future,* ed. N. Polunin (London: Macmillan and Co., 1972), pp. 181–211.

2. *Final Report on Phase I of Water Policy Implementation,* Report Submitted to the President by the Secretary of the Interior, June 6, 1980, pp. iii–iv.

3. W. Viessman, Jr. and C. DeMoncada, *State and National Water Use Trends to the Year 2000,* a report prepared by the Congressional Research Service for the U.S. Senate, Serial No. 96–12, (Washington, D.C.: U.S. Government Printing Office, 1980), pp. 257–59. These figures represent a national average; estimates vary from about 118 gallons per capita to the more often quoted 250 gallons per day *consumed* by a family of four.

4. *The Groundwater Newsletter* 11, no. 5 (1982); *Water/Engineering and Management* 129, no. 3 (1982):22.

5. W. G. Characklis, et al., *Maximum Utilization of Water Resources in a Planned Community,* EPA–600/2–79–050a (Washington, D.C.: Environmental Protection Agency, 1979).

6. S. A. Roberts and S. K. Krishnaswami, "Protecting the Source," *Water/Engineering and Management* 129, no. 3 (1982):28–31.

7. Ibid.

8. Cf. J. Wilhm et al., *Diagnostic-feasibility Study of Lake Carl Blackwell,* EPA S–006291–01–0 (Washington, D.C.: Environmental Protection Agency, 1980). Many such studies have been completed under the EPA Clean

Lakes Program, all of which suggest that shoreline modification is an important part of lake restoration.

9. S. H. Wittwer, "The Blue Revolution," *Natural History* 88, no. 9 (1979):8–18.

10. Interagency Task Force, *Irrigation Water Use and Management,* (Washington, D.C.: U.S. Government Printing Office, 1979), pp. 1–10.

11. Report by Jack Stone to Conference on Horizons in Water Research, Water Research Institute, Oklahoma State University, Stillwater, Oklahoma, April, 1982.

12. Interagency Task Force, *Irrigation Water Use and Management,* pp. 1–10, 13.

13. Ibid., p. 4.

14. J. Neary, "Pickleweed, Palmer's Grass, and Saltwort: Can We Grow Tomorrow's Food with Today's Salt Water?" *Science* 81 (June 1981):39–43. D. Sheridan, "The Underwatered West: Overdrawn at the Well," *Environment* 23, no. 2 (1981):6–33.

15. H. C. Chang, A. L. Page, and F. T. Bingham, "Reutilization of Municipal Wastewater Sludges—Metals and Nitrate," *Journal of Water Pollution Control Federation* 53, no. 2 (1981):237–45.

16. Chang, Page, and Bingham, "Reutilization of Municipal Wastewater." These arguments were also summarized in a feature report of an important conference on wastewater management held in Oklahoma City in 1974. Its recommendations were published in *Fisheries* 2, no. 1 (1976):19, 44. In a thirteen-point proposal, the conference members drew up a usable strategy for wastewater reuse which, although scientifically and economically sound, has yet to be widely applied.

17. H. H. McMillan, R. R. Rimkus, and F. C. Neil, "Metro Chicago's Study of Energy Alternatives for Wastewater Treatment," *Journal of Water Pollution Control Federation* 53, no. 2 (1981):155–61.

18. U.S. Environmental Protection Agency, *Process Design Manual for Land Treatment of Municipal Wastewater,* EPA 625/1–77–008 (Washington, D.C.: Office of Water Program Operations, 1977).

19. A. R. Overman, *Wastewater Irrigation at Tallahassee, Florida,* EPA–600/2–79–151 (Springfield, Vir.: National Technical Information Service, 1979).

20. D. H. Hall and J. E. Shelton, *Municipal Wastewater Treatment by the Overland Flow Method of Land Application,* EPA–600/2–79–178 (Springfield, Vir.: National Technical Information Service, 1979).

21. E. L. Koerner and D. A. Haus, *Long-term Effects of Land Application of Domestic Wastewater—Roswell, New Mexico, Slow Rate Irrigation Site,* EPA–600/2–79–047, (Springfield, Vir.: National Technical Information Service, 1979).

22. P. Stubblefield, "Water for Crops, not Waste," *Tulsa World,* May 17, 1982, p. 7.

23. Advisory Panel on Agricultural Water Conservation, State of California, May, 1979, p. 6.

24. Quoted in J. Risser, "A Renewal Threat of Soil Erosion: It's Worse Than the Dust Bowl," *Smithsonian* 11, no. 12 (1981):120–30.

25. S. A. Spigarelli, "Legacy of a Thirsty Society," *Natural History* 87, no. 7 (1978):76–79.

26. Viessman and DeMoncada, "State and National Water Use Trends," pp. 250–57.

27. Ibid., p. 254. Also summarized in *Water Policies for the Future* (Washington, D.C.: U.S. Government Printing Office, 1978).

28. Viessman and DeMoncada, "State and National Water Use Trends," pp. 259–62. See also original data in U.S. Water Resources Council, *Water for Energy—Supplemental Report to the Second National Assessment* (Washington, D.C.: U.S. Government Printing Office, 1978).

29. N. D. Baratta, W. T. Grandin, and M. Prescott, "Industrial Waste Cooperatives—Are They Feasible?" *Public Works* 112, no. 9 (1981):106–9.

30. Report to the Conference on Horizons in Water Research, Water Research Institute, Oklahoma State University, Stillwater, Oklahoma, April, 1982.

31. Final Report on Phase I of Water Policy Implementation, Appendix A.

Glossary

Acre foot the amount of water required to cover an acre of land one foot deep; about 325,851 U.S. gallons

Aquifer a geologic formation, group of formations, or part of a formation that is water yielding

Brackish water water containing dissolved minerals (1,000–10,000 mg/liter) in excess of potable water standards but less than that of sea water

Brine a highly mineralized solution (usually greater than 100,000 mg/liter), especially of chloride salts, often produced as a waste product of desalination of sea water

Buffering capacity the ability of a solution or system, such as lake water or soil moisture, to resist changes. An example is bicarbonate in water that is capable of neutralizing both added acids and bases and thereby maintaining the original acidity or basicity of the solution

Carrying capacity the upper limit of a system to support all components within the resources available

Coliform bacteria a group of bacteria commonly found in the intestines of higher animals, including man, indicative in water of fecal contamination

Cone of depression a depression in a water table, approximately cone-shaped, resulting from groundwater withdrawal or overdraft

Consumptive use that part of water withdrawn which is no longer available for use because it has either evaporated, transpired, been incorporated into products, or otherwise removed from the water environment

Contamination any degradation of natural water quality caused by man's activities

Degradation in water, any process that reduces the quality of a water source

Demophoric growth a concept of growth which combines the effects of both increased human population numbers with the increased consumption of resources resulting from expanding technology

Desalination the energy-requiring process by which dissolved salts are removed from water

Drawdown a process of lowering the water levels in reservoirs

Ecotone a transition zone between two or more diverse communities, e.g., between forest and grassland

Effluent a waste liquid that discharges into the environment

Eutrophication an enriched condition of aquatic ecosystems characterized by increased production of certain plants and animals, reduced types of plants and animals, and a reduction in the ability of many organisms to resist changes in the environment

Evapotranspiration loss of water from the soil both by evaporation and by transpiration from the plants growing upon it

Groundwater water beneath the land surface stored in a saturated zone in geologic strata

Hazardous waste any waste discharged into the environment which possesses a present or potential danger to humans, other animals, or plants

Heavy metals metallic elements required for plant and animal nutrition but which become toxic at higher levels; examples are copper, mercury, cadmium, and lead

Hydrological cycle the cyclic processes of water movements from the atmosphere, its inflow and temporary storage on and in land, and its outflow to the oceans. The cycle consists of three principal phases: precipitation, evaporation, and surface and groundwater runoff

Infiltration a flow of liquid into soil or rock through pores or small openings

Leachate a liquid that has percolated through solid waste or other man-emplaced media and has extracted dissolved or suspended material from it

Littoral zone the shoreline or coastal region of lakes that extends from the area of water-saturated soils down into the lake to the boundary where light no longer reaches the underwater sediments

Morphometry the form and shape characteristics of lake basins and stream channels and their measurement

Nonpoint source a contaminant source which emits wastes in a diffuse or intermittent manner

Nutrients compounds of nitrogen, phosphorus, or other elements required for organismal growth

Overdraft the process of removing more from a supply than is really available for the purpose intended for the supply

Percolation movement under hydrostatic pressure of water through unsaturated rock or soil

Point source a confined or defined source of water contamination

Pollutant any substance which becomes dissolved in water and impairs its usefulness

Pore an open space in rock or soil

Potable water of a suitable quality for drinking without harmful effects

Recharge the addition of water to a ground or surface water system by natural or artifical processes

Retention time the period of time that water remains in a given reservoir (lake, stream, as vapor in the atmosphere, etc.)

Runoff direct or overland flow of rainfall not absorbed by soil, evaporated, or transpired by plants, thus finding its way into streams or surface flow

Safe yield an acceptable maximum limit of use or amount of pollution to the environment that can be tolerated for multipurpose uses of the environment by humans

Salt water intrusion movement of saline water into groundwater previously containing fresh water

Saturated   all voids of a substance or situation are completely filled by some other substance or component, e.g., the most concentrated situation in soils where voids between soil particles are filled with water

Saturated zone   soil or rock strata saturated with water

Sinkholes   a depression in which water collects and which commonly results from land collapsing into an underground cavern created by removal of supporting water formerly contained in it

Surface water   water stored on the land surface, including lakes, rivers, streams, and oceans

Toxicity   the ability of a material to produce injury or disease in a living organism upon exposure

Transpiration   the process by which water passes as water vapor from organisms, especially plants, through membranes or pores to the atmosphere

Water quality   the chemical, physical, and biological properties of water and their suitability for a particular purpose

Water renewal   the amount of water required to replace the lake volume during a given time interval

Watershed   the drainage area or region bounded by water flow to a particular stream system or body of water

Water table   the surface of an unconfined groundwater body, defining the top of the saturated zone

Index